The CaReeR CowaRd's Guide™ to Resumes

Sensible Strategies for Overcoming Job Search Fears

Katy Piotrowski, M.Ed.

The Career Coward's Guide to Resumes

© 2008 by Katy Piotrowski

Published by JIST Works, an imprint of JIST Publishing
7321 Shadeland Station, Suite 200
Indianapolis, IN 46256-3923
Phone: 800-648-JIST   Fax: 877-454-7839   E-mail: info@jist.com

Visit our Web site at **www.jist.com** for information on JIST, free job search tips, tables of contents and sample chapters, and ordering instructions for our many products!

See the back of this book for additional JIST titles and ordering information. Quantity discounts are available for JIST books. Have future editions of JIST books automatically delivered to you on publication through our convenient standing order program. Please call our Sales Department at 800-648-5478 for a free catalog and more information.

Trade Product Manager: Lori Cates Hand
Cover Designer: Trudy Coler
Illustrator: Chris Sabatino
Interior Designer: Amy Adams
Page Layout: Toi Davis
Proofreaders: Paula Lowell, Jeanne Clark
Indexer: Cheryl Lenser

Printed in the United States of America
13 12 11 10 09 08   9 8 7 6 5 4 3 2

    Library of Congress Cataloging-in-Publication Data
Piotrowski, Katy, 1962-
    The career coward's guide to resumes : sensible strategies for overcoming job search fears / by Katy Piotrowski.
        p. cm.
    Includes index.
    ISBN-13: 978-1-59357-391-1 (alk. paper)
    1. Résumés (Employment) I. Title.
    HF5383.P535 2008
    650.14'2--dc22
                                        2007046921

We have been careful to provide accurate information in this book, but it is possible that errors and omissions have been introduced. Please consider this in making any career plans or other important decisions. Trust your own judgment above all else and in all things.

ISBN 978-1-59357-391-1

About This Book

Creating a resume for yourself can feel like an overwhelming project: "What should I include? How should I describe myself? What format should I use? How do I overcome the little glitches in my career?" may be just a few of the questions you're wrestling with right now.

But since you're holding this book in your hands, feel free to take a deep breath and lower your stress level a few notches, because you now have an excellent, step-by-step, "you can do it!" guide to walk you through the process.

Over the last several years, I've helped thousands of real people—people experiencing the same challenges you face—create effective resumes that helped them achieve their career goals. The questions those people have asked, the struggles they've encountered, and the successes they accomplished are described in this book...right down to the nitty-gritty details of how many years of experience to include, what to do if you feel as if you *have* no experience in an important area, how to handle gaps in your career timeline, and more.

This in-depth, real-world information has been boiled down into a doable, step-by-step process that will allow you to create dynamite resumes and cover letters that produce the results you want.

Still not convinced *The Career Coward's Guide to Resumes* is for you? Take a few seconds to flip through the book and look at some of the examples presented. When you follow the recommendations in this book, you'll be able to produce resumes like that, too. Also take a peek at the Panic Points (the highlighted paragraphs in each chapter) that describe scary situations that job searchers often encounter. Solid, effective solutions are provided for every Panic Point situation.

And because I know that writing a resume can feel like hard work, I've made sure that each recommendation is clear and doable, as well as provided you encouraging suggestions along the way.

So let's take your success to the next level and work together to build resumes that move you forward in your career. Just turn the page to get started!

—Katy P.

Dedication

To Jim C., who taught me how to promote people and products though words, and to Louise K., who is an inspiration to me.

Contents

Acknowledgments

First and foremost, I want to thank the clients who have allowed me the honor of working with them on their career projects. Their challenges are a constant motivation for me to keep learning, and their successes bring so much joy and meaning to my life. I'd also like to thank my husband, Pete, who continues to encourage and support me in the work I love so much; my editor, Lori, whose expertise and guidance have resulted in books that I'm proud to call my own; my publicists, Natalie and Selena, who know how to have fun while moving us forward; the career and counseling gurus who have been so important in my work, especially Nathalie Kees, Rich Feller, Daniel Porot, Richard Knowdell, and Dick Bolles; the writing experts who have been teachers and models for me, specifically Jim Caron and Louise Kursmark; and my friends and family—you are so important to me!

Tame the Coward and Write Your Resume!

Welcome to *The Career Coward's Guide to Resumes*, a powerful guide designed to lead you successfully (and fearlessly) through the process of building resumes and other job search documents that support achievement of your career goals. The suggestions provided in this book have been acquired and refined through the development of thousands of real-world resumes over the past 15 years. You can feel confident in the recommendations presented in this book because they work! Have fun (and push through your fears) as you develop resumes that move you closer to achieving your career dreams.

How to Use This Book to Achieve Your Resume and Career Goals

The Career Coward's Guide to Resumes will walk you through a proven, step-by-step process for overcoming your challenges and concerns, resulting in the creation of powerful resumes. Each chapter in *The Career Coward's Guide to Resumes* will provide you with techniques that have been tried, tested, and perfected on thousands of other Career Cowards. And to make this valuable information even more fun and easy to use, each chapter includes an at-a-glance "Risk It or Run From It" status box, providing you the following vital information:

- **Risk Rating:** From "No risk at all" to "This is a deal breaker!" you'll quickly see how harmless or hazardous each step will be.

- **Payoff Potential:** Find out what's in it for you if you decide to take the risk and complete the step. The payoff may be enough to push you through any fear holding you back.

- **Time to Complete:** Whether it's a few minutes, a few hours, or longer, you'll know in advance how much time each activity will take.

- **Bailout Strategy:** Absolutely refuse to put in the time or take the risk for a particular step? You have other options; find out what they are.

- **The "20 Percent Extra" Edge:** Learn how braving the recommended steps will give you a significant advantage over your competition.

- **"Go for It!" Bonus Activity:** Feeling really courageous? Push your success even further with this suggested activity.

Each information-packed chapter also includes the following:

- A "How To" section, providing clear, motivating instructions for each activity.

- Information about "Why It's Worth Doing," helping you to understand the purpose behind each resume-building recommendation.

- "Panic Point!" highlights, pointing out and troubleshooting areas Career Cowards find especially challenging.

- An encouraging "Career Champ Profile," describing a real-life example of a Career Coward who succeeded after conquering resume challenges, along with an example of his or her resume (names, addresses, and contact information have been changed to protect privacy).

- The "Core Courage Concept," boiling down the chapter's key points into an inspiring message.

- And a "Confidence Checklist," providing you an at-a-glance review of the chapter's primary action items.

As you move through the chapters of this book, you'll learn how to implement and succeed with the following proven resume-building action plan:

- You'll begin by gaining an in-depth understanding of the purpose for a resume, as well as learning more about a hiring manager's priorities related to the information you're presenting.

- From there, you'll decide on a focus for your resume, helping you to simplify the process for choosing which information to include and how to best present it.

- As a next step, you'll conduct some initial research into the keywords and phrasing most important to include in your resume, based on your chosen career target.

- Moving forward, you'll scope out how best to present your work history, education, and "extras" information, based on your unique situation.

- Your next step will be to decide which resume format will best serve your career goals. A range of effective formats and a helpful survey are provided to help with your decision making. You'll then pull together your information into the format most ideal for your situation.

- Formatting and polishing your resume will happen next, allowing you to promote your qualifications and experience to their best advantage.

- When your resume document is completed, you'll learn proven strategies for creating powerful cover letters, thank you notes, references listings, and portfolios.

- And as a final step, you'll find out how to effectively launch your outstanding job search documents into the job market to achieve the best results.

Eager to get started? Great! Read about the successes of one former Career Coward and then launch into creating a Career Champ story of your own....

Career Champ Profile: Carina

Carina had achieved many successes in her marketing career, most recently with an employer with whom she loved working. But then the company announced that it would be relocating to another state, and Carina didn't want to move. At first Carina panicked. How would she ever be able to communicate her skills and accomplishments in a resume that would allow her to land another great position? Yet, after catching her breath and calming her fears, Carina was able to follow the steps outlined in this process and create a resume that generated outstanding results immediately. Within just a few weeks, her resume helped her land a terrific position with another wonderful employer.

Carina Wilson   *Marketing Program Manager*

2441 Lovely Street, Fort Collins, CO
970.416.5555 • email@peakpeak.com

Expert Communications Program Management

Accomplished **Marketing Programs Developer, Implementer, and Manager** with expertise in leading multiple initiatives from start to finish; proven success working effectively with peers, agencies, corporate marketing, business units, and IT to manage marketing messaging for Internet and website projects, data analysis and reporting, and market research and database marketing; outstanding track record for managing projects to meet established cost- and timeline objectives; creative, hands-on, web-savvy, team player with exceptional organizational and communication skills; proven success implementing emerging technologies, with expertise in Microsoft NT environments, HTML, XML, JavaScript, and PowerPoint.

RELATED ACCOMPLISHMENTS

➢ **Successfully managed development and launch of 1,000-page, $250k web portal project** involving migration to new server technology. Managed plan, teams, budgets, reporting, troubleshooting, and accountability for a flawless launch, leading to outstanding program results.

➢ **Achieved reputation as an outstanding program and team manager,** resulting in long-term, productive working relationships with team members and consistent, efficient achievement of marketing objectives.

➢ **Developed a highly effective project tracking methodology** resulting in accurate reporting on project costs and status. System allows for timely troubleshooting of problems and higher levels of program success.

PROFESSIONAL EXPERIENCE

Marketing Project Manager/Account Manager — *Fantastic Employer, Inc.*   2000–present
- Manage multiple enterprise-level web portals and web development projects with budgets of up to $2 million, and teams of up to 20 copywriters, webmasters, designers, and application developers.
- Develop project proposals, SOWs, budgets, timelines, invoices, and out-of-scope change orders and drive creative and technical project delivery processes following standard project lifecycle.
- Enforce stringent content quality assurance processes and produce detailed weekly and monthly reports covering hours, costs, forecasts, and project status.

Product Marketing Project Manager — *Great Place to Work,* 1999–2000
- Developed and managed product marketing, including worldwide packaging strategy planning and product documentation programs, and deliverables for new product launches.
- Developed and maintained competitive analysis reports for sales and marketing teams.

Graduate Student, Master of Arts in Marketing Communications, *University of Colorado,* 1997–1998

Production Coordinator/Graphic Designer — *Organization Extraordinaire,* 1995–1997
- Designed and managed advertising, resume, and collateral projects and schedules.
- Managed client relationships and accounts, and a team of seven graphic designers.

Additional experience managing publications and printing. Details provided on request.

EDUCATION

Master of Arts — **Marketing Communications** — University of Colorado
Bachelor of Arts — **English** — University of Oregon

Figure I.1: Carina's resume.

Part 1

Lay the Foundations for a Successful Resume

Chapter 1

Learn the Basics of Resume-Writing Success

C'mon, admit it. You've laid in bed several nights imagining what it would be like to have an employer receive your resume and excitedly call you to arrange an interview…to meet with her and have her offer you your dream job at great pay…to go to work day after day and love what you're doing.

But then reality hits. You're stuck on the first step: You don't have a great resume to send to an employer. The other pieces won't come together until you can get past the resume hurdle. And until now, you've struggled with how to put together an awesome resume document. Lucky you, though! You've picked up the right resource to walk you through the process. Step by step, you'll create a resume that will help you achieve your dream.

Risk It or Run From It?

- **Risk Rating:** No risk here. You're just learning the basics for effective resume creation.

(continued)

(continued)

- **Payoff Potential:** Big! After you gain an overview of the key considerations involved in putting together your resume, you'll better understand how to structure your resume for success.

- **Time to Complete:** A few minutes. You'll be done in no time.

- **Bailout Strategy:** Turn directly to chapter 3 and begin building your resume immediately. However, if later in this book you're asking yourself, "What's the purpose of this piece...or this one?" then flip back here to help put things in perspective.

- **The "20 Percent Extra" Edge:** Understanding the theory behind creating a successful resume will save you from wasted time and effort down the line.   ‾

- **"Go for It!" Bonus Activity:** As I describe the concepts behind building a successful document, flip through the resume examples in this book to see how we've accomplished these objectives. This step will give you more information about how to effectively develop your own.

How to Set Yourself Up for Resume-Writing Success

Remember the last time you bought a big-ticket item, like a car, house, or even a cell phone? When you did, you probably spent some time reading up about it before you made your purchase. If it was a car, you may have looked through the auto dealer's slick brochure, soaking up the information that interested you. Or with a cell phone, you may have surfed the Internet comparing providers and phone styles. Whatever it was, you most likely sought out some background information about the item before signing on the bottom line.

Marketing departments at companies producing those big-ticket items know that before consumers buy, they want to study some written material describing the product or service. So they put together brochures and Web pages to help people access the data they need. And those marketing specialists are very thoughtful about what they present to you. They want you to have a "Wow, I want to see more!" reaction when you read their brochure or view their Web page.

View Yourself as a "Big-Ticket Item"

Similar to a car or house, you are now a big-ticket item, and you're getting ready to put yourself on the market. Just as car manufacturers put together a brochure and Web page, you need to put together some written material (your resume!) that generates a "Wow, I want to see more!" response from a potential employer. Seems like a tall order to fill, doesn't it? But in reality, it's not rocket science. Just as marketing specialists around the world have figured out how to highlight the right kind of information to motivate buyers, you, too, can use a proven success formula to build a resume that generates excitement and interest.

Factor Key Success Concepts into Your Resume Planning

These are some key elements you'll want to factor into the results-producing resume you create:

1. A target for your resume. Where does your expertise and background best fit, and who are the employers who will be most interested in you? For instance, truck manufacturers produce heavy-duty machines that can handle rugged tasks. They market those vehicles to men who like to haul things and perform manly jobs. Advertising a Chevy half-ton pickup to a soccer mom with four kids wouldn't be a good use of their time and money. So, as a start, I'll spend some time helping you focus on career positions that are the best fit for you.

2. Relevant aspects of your background. Which parts of your experience will be most interesting to your target employers? Again, using the car analogy, Toyota knows that a soccer mom with four kids will often have her hands full, so a single press of a button to open the minivan door will be appealing to her. Toyota prominently displays that feature in its TV ads and

brochures. I'll walk you through a proven process to identify your own best features and ways to emphasize them.

3. The perception that you're a "reasonable risk." How will you communicate to a hiring manager that you're predictable and reliable? Just as you wouldn't buy a junker car that looks as if it won't make it around the block, the person reading your resume wants to believe that you'll be dependable, just by looking at your resume. You'll learn effective techniques to convey your solid performance to future employers—even if you have a few holes in your background.

4. Features that motivate the resume screener to take action. What will make your resume stand out from the 100+ other resumes in the pile? One of this year's new Volkswagen Beetle colors may be just what it takes to get a potential car buyer to the car lot. You'll want to include some sexy, excitement-building features into your resume to get the hiring manager moving as well.

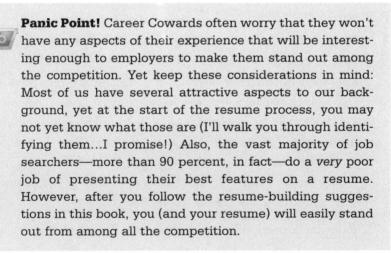

Panic Point! Career Cowards often worry that they won't have any aspects of their experience that will be interesting enough to employers to make them stand out among the competition. Yet keep these considerations in mind: Most of us have several attractive aspects to our background, yet at the start of the resume process, you may not yet know what those are (I'll walk you through identifying them...I promise!) Also, the vast majority of job searchers—more than 90 percent, in fact—do a *very* poor job of presenting their best features on a resume. However, after you follow the resume-building suggestions in this book, you (and your resume) will easily stand out from among all the competition.

So beginning now, I'd like you to think like a marketer aiming to sell a big-ticket item—yourself!—to a qualified buyer. As you review the effective resume-writing techniques I describe in this book, do your best to view yourself as a product for sale—rather than a person looking for a job. This approach will help you be more objective and successful in making choices about what to include (or not to include) in your resume.

And before you know it, you'll be sending out your own "brochure," motivating potential buyers to want to know more about you!

Why It's Worth Doing

In my lifetime, I've looked at tens of thousands of resumes. The vast majority (I'd guess about 80 percent of them) are simply lists of pieces of information about a candidate's background. There appears to be no thought regarding the kind of position the job seeker is aiming for and what a potential employer would be interested in knowing related to that person's background. Only a few are targeted, well organized, and fun to read. The rest are a drudge to get through.

Now imagine what it's like to be a recruiter, looking at more than a thousand resumes *each week!* Or a hiring manager, working through a stack of 100 to 200 resumes with the goal of finding some candidates to interview. These people literally spend only 7 to 10 seconds initially scanning applicant backgrounds. If a resume doesn't quickly convey the key pieces of information screeners are looking for, they move on to the next.

Yet in a way, all these poorly written resumes are good news for you. Because so few people know how to put together an effective document, the techniques you learn and apply from this book will easily position you above your competition. It's definitely worthwhile to learn successful resume-development techniques at this point, to help you land your next position, and to support future advancements in your career.

Career Champ Profile: Karla

When I talked with Karla, she'd been miserable in her job for almost two years. Although she was happy working for her present employers for more than 10 years, changes at the company over the past several months were causing her lots of frustrations. She was definitely ready to find a new job.

"How will I show everything I know in just a page or two?" she asked me with a worried expression on her face. "Let's start with the basics," I encouraged her. What kind of work are you hoping to find?" She answered that she wanted another position as a financial controller. "It's a great fit for me. I love knowing what's going on financially all around the company." "Good!" I responded. "Now tell me, what are the most important qualifications necessary to be a successful controller?"

Karla told me that an effective controller has to be good with numbers. "My degree is accounting," she explained. "A good controller also needs to be able to see how all of the pieces of the company work together, and to develop processes, like computer information systems, so that things can run smoothly and efficiently." And lastly, Karla told me that a successful financial controller has to have strong people skills. "When you're telling the vice president of manufacturing that he's over on his budget, you need to do so tactfully, or it can be a nightmare!" she said laughing.

"Are you experienced in all of these areas?" I asked her next. She nodded her head yes. "Would you be able to give me specific examples of times when you've completed projects or had successes in these skill areas?" I continued. "Yes, lots!" she said, smiling broadly.

"Then guess what?" I said, laughing. "You've already done all of the hard work. Now we just need to put these pieces of information into your resume!" This was the result:

Karla Mitchell-Sadler

400 Plane Drive, Fort Collins, CO 80526, (970) 555-6666, karla_mitchell_sadler@email.com

CONTROLLER / OPERATIONS

Results-oriented Finance & Operations Professional with extensive experience in financial reporting, analysis, forecasting, budgeting, cash management, and controls for manufacturing and industrial organization. Possess solid interpersonal skills and cross-functional team interactions (Sales, Manufacturing, Information Systems, etc.); offer a proven track record for reorganizing, streamlining, and strengthening operations to maximize performance and profitability; Adept at effectively interpreting and translating business needs into system requirements; able to exercise sound judgment in selecting methods for business solutions. *Expertise:*

- A/R, A/P, & G /L Account Analysis
- Financial Statements & Reporting
- Process Analysis & Improvement
- Banking & Insurance Management

- Information Systems Development
- Automated Financial Systems Software
- Inventory Management & Reconciliation
- Staff Training & Development

WORK HISTORY

Metalwork Industries
Oversee Accounting, Inventory, and Information Systems processes for nationwide manufacturer and distributor of welding and metalworking products with $40 million in annual sales.

Controller / Operations, 1996–Present *(Assistant Controller, 1996–1998)*
- Oversee A/R, A/P, G/L, Payroll, Inventory, and Sales Journals, and perform Journal Entries, Cash Flow, Fixed Assets, Investment Analysis, and Accrued Liabilities.
- Direct Information Systems planning and implementation for continuous performance improvements.
- Handle monthly- and year-end closings including reconciliations, analyze financial information, prepare financial reports, and verify accuracy of calculations and postings.
- Plan, direct, and coordinate operational activities to comply with accounting standards and tax reporting laws, and determine and formulate policies and business strategies.

....**Highlights of Achievements**..
- ✓ Transformed costly hard-copy invoicing system, generating more than 130,000 six-part forms annually, to paperless Web-based operation, **resulting in $150k in annual cost savings.**
- ✓ **Oversaw highly successful retraining of more than 150 company employees,** many of whom had little or no computer skills, to support transition to improved automated systems.
- ✓ Renegotiated shipping contract, **saving organization more than $400k per year.**
- ✓ Researched and implemented high-quality, low-cost employee benefits programs.

America Invests, Financial Planner, 2004–2006 *(part-time)*

EDUCATION, CERTIFICATIONS, AFFILIATIONS

- **B.S. Business Administration,** Colorado State University, *Cost Accounting Emphasis*
- **Certifications:** MS Office: Excel, Access, Word, Outlook, PowerPoint; DataWatch Monarch; Crystal Reports; Stellent Imaging Business Manager; Sterling Commerce Director Pro Integration
- **Affiliations:** National Society of Accountants, Executive Women's Golf Association

Figure 1.1: Karla's resume.

Core Courage Concept

When you first think about writing a resume, wondering how you'll choose and put together hundreds of pieces of information to create a successful result can be overwhelming. Yet as with most things in life, when you cover the basics, the rest of the pieces fall in place more easily. Sure, you'll experience a few moments of panic as you work through the process of writing your resume. When you do, remind yourself that you have great experience and skills to offer and that you need to just take things one step at a time.

Confidence Checklist

- ☐ View yourself as a "big-ticket item."
- ☐ Factor key success concepts into your resume planning.

Chapter 2

Find Out What Hiring Managers Want in Your Resume

You've already acquired a basic understanding of the key concepts you'll want to convey with your resume. Now let's take a minute to understand more about the decision maker's perspective. Knowing the priorities and challenges of resume screeners, recruiters, and hiring managers will give you an inside advantage to planning and creating resumes that deliver excellent results for you.

Risk It or Run From It?

- **Risk Rating:** None. You're just reading and learning.

- **Payoff Potential:** Very, very high. Understanding more about the resume review process from the resume screener's perspective will give you a huge advantage.

- **Time to Complete:** Just a few minutes.

- **Bailout Strategy:** Skip ahead to chapter 3 and dive into building your resume.

(continued)

(continued)

- **The "20 Percent Extra" Edge:** Knowing more about how your resume is viewed from a decision maker's perspective allows you to develop resumes with a much greater chance of getting the results you want.

- **"Go for It!" Bonus Activity:** Talk with any decision makers you know—managers, supervisors, recruiters—and ask them what they look for when reading a resume. Their answers will provide you an even greater insight into how to set up your resume for success.

How to Give Resume Screeners What They Want

We all know the story of Goldilocks, wandering into the bears' home in search of food and rest. After many frustrating "too big" or "too small" attempts, Goldy finally finds the porridge, chair, and bed that are "just right" for her. Happily, her needs are met.

In your job search, your aim is to help the decision maker find the "Just Right!" resume—yours! If you already have a resume, what kinds of results are you getting with it? If your results are poor, you may be using a document that's either Too Big or Too Small. Read the following descriptions to see which label best fits your resume style.

The Too-Small Resume

A Too-Small Resume is typically one page, made up of short-phrase listings. Job searchers using a Too-Small Resume often believe that less is more. A few key details—most likely their name, address, and phone number; a list of previous and current employers; and a few words describing education—and they deem their resume as good to go. Who wants to spend more than a minute reading a resume, right? So the Too-Small Resume users think they're helping out the resume screener by providing minimal details.

Ann Toosmall
400 Indian Lane
Salisbury, MD 21801
(410)555-3333 ann.patrick@yahoo.com

Work History

Customer Service Representative, ABC Company, March 2006–Present
Answer questions and provide product information to customers.

Receptionist, XYZ Company, June 2003–February 2006
Answered phones, scheduled appointments, handled filing and paperwork.

Bank Teller, LMNOP Bank, September 2000–May 2003
Made deposits and withdrawals. Balanced cash drawer.

Education

Three classes at Mountain Peaks Community College
Graduate, Bennett Senior High School

Figure 2.1: A Too-Small Resume.

In reality, however, when a hiring manager reviews a Too-Small Resume, he or she is often left feeling hungry for more information. "This is a good start," the decision maker may think, "but I need more details to feel like this person is worth interviewing." Up against a Just-Right Resume, the job searchers with a Too-Small Resume come across as inexperienced or disinterested. "I really didn't have any relevant background to describe" or "I'm too busy to take the time to give you the information you need" is the message they risk sending.

The Too-Big Resume

A Too-Big Resume usually runs on for at least two pages and often tops out at four or more. Job hunters with a Too-Big Resume typically believe that the hiring manager will want to know *everything* about their background, in case there's a special skill or quality that might be useful. They picture hiring managers carefully reading through all the information in a resume, combing through the details to gain a solid picture of an applicant's qualifications. As a result, they believe it's important to describe *all* their experience, beginning with their first job in high school, so that the decision maker will know the full extent of their abilities. "If I leave out an element of a job description or training course, I run the risk of leaving out the very detail that might have made the difference, right?"

Wrong! Although some very conscientious hiring managers diligently study all the data in resumes, the vast majority of resume screeners just skim the information looking for highlights. In fact, on average, a decision maker will spend just 7 to 10 seconds giving your resume an initial scan. If they can't find what they're looking for quickly, chances are that your Too-Big Resume will be placed in the "No Way!" pile, leaving the reviewer with a sour, "That was too much work!" taste in his or her mouth.

The Just-Right Resume

A Just-Right Resume is almost always one to two pages long. The searchers using a Just-Right Resume understand that a decision maker's time is valuable, and that it's the job hunter's responsibility to clearly communicate adequate information in a minimal amount of time. Just-Right Resume users know that chances are very good that their resume will be one of more than 100 that the screener is reviewing. To help their resume stand out among those 100+, these searchers aim to include only relevant information and to present it in a format that's visually appealing and easy to read.

When a hiring manager reads a Just-Right Resume, he or she experiences a feeling of relief and excitement. The manager's reaction is usually, "This candidate looks good! I see the key pieces of information I'm looking for, and I found that info quickly and easily. This candidate seems to understand my needs. I want to learn more about this person." Often, this leads to a call for an interview—just the result the job seeker is hoping for.

Jeff Toobig

2751 River Run Rd.   (c) 970.888.3333
Ft. Collins, CO 80526   (w) 970.888.4444
jeff.toobig@comcast.net

PROFILE:
*** 2005–Feb 2007 Owned and operated a franchise restaurant concurrent with my Big
Computer Company responsibilities. See last page for details.

Big Computer Company, Ft. Collins, CO, 2005–current
As **Software QA Program Manager,** I am responsible for monitoring, assessing, and managing the
incoming defect streams for concurrent BCUX enterprise software releases. It is my job to represent
the USEL software lab at daily defect review meetings which assess the overall fitness of each BCUX
release. I then follow up across multiple software development projects with tactics for ensuring each
release meets schedule and quality goals as determined by the program team on which I sit. In this
role I interact with all program levels in the lab from software engineer through lab manager. I am
often called upon to mediate cross-functional "swat" teams which interact to solve critical defects for
which there is no clear team ownership. It is also my job to statically debug kernel crash dumps to
determine a root cause for each defect submitted against the BCUX kernel and then forward the
defects along with my analyses to the correct lab teams for execution of fixes. Following the 11.31
BCUX enterprise release, my role has expanded to include management of key areas of our lab-wide
transition from our legacy defect tracking system to a BC standard defect tracking system. This
transition will take place over two fiscal quarters and will entail transition of over 200,000 active and
archived defects.

WORK EXPERIENCE

Big Computer Company, Ft. Collins, CO, 2002–2005
As **Software Engineering Project Manager,** I was responsible for leading, planning, and managing
the development and maintenance of enterprise software applications as well as enterprise software
development environments through the entire software development life cycle. I have extensive
experience with project team development and reinvention through the management and leadership
of engineering teams (up to 17 engineers), including recruiting, retention, reduction, reward, and
professional development/coaching. As part of Software R&D I have had extensive partnering
experience with Quality Assurance, Information Engineering, Operations, Product Development,
Global Support, Current Product Engineering, Technical Marketing, Expert Centers, Contract
Negotiations, and Human Resources to define and implement project plans. Specific experience
includes setting strategic direction and vision, gathering and refining requirements, defining project
scope, schedule estimation, project plan creation, managing design and implementation, resource
allocation, work breakdown and prioritization, and releasing quality products as well as quality
software delivery processes. I have performed risk analysis and contingency planning. I have
established and maintained project schedules to ensure on-time product delivery. I have worked
closely with all levels of management from technical leads through R&D Vice President to define
and deliver software projects as well as promote and implement best practices and processes
throughout engineering. My management experience includes influencing, partnering, and leading
engineers and managers that span multiple cultures including American, German, French, and
Japanese. I have also had experience managing and leading engineering teams that span multiple
geographies.

Figure 2.2: A Too-Big Resume.

(continued)

(continued)

As **Software Engineering Project Manager**, I led and managed an engineering team split across multiple geographies to investigate, implement, design, deploy, and support a new installation system across the entire BC OpenUse enterprise management product line. This system included tool sets, programs, and process to reinvent the entire installation paradigm across the OpenUse lab. Support for this program was garnered via extensive communication and lobbying at all levels of OpenUse management from project manager through R&D manager. Deployment was achieved via pilot programs executed in conjunction with the delivery schedules of several key OpenUse products. All phases of product delivery came in on time and within 10% of extremely tight budgetary constraints.

As **Software Engineering Project Manager**, I led, managed, and delivered a three-year project focused on the creation of a software delivery system between Big Computer Company and Hattrick Inc. that completely renovated the way these two companies exchange source code. Managing this project required a great deal of face-to-face negotiating with Japanese management regarding feature sets and project scoping. Project visibility extended through the senior vice president level. This project was delivered in phases with each phase coming in on time. Escalations were completely avoided by continual hands-on management of both BC's and Hattrick's leadership teams.

Big Computer Company, Ft. Collins, CO, 2001–2002

As **Software Solutions Architect,** I created and delivered the solution architecture used for the BC-Clickon-Software.com Unified Communications project and managed all aspects of the technical partner relationships across functional and corporate lines.

Big Computer Company, Ft. Collins, CO, 1998–2001

As **Senior Software Engineer,** I led an engineering team that designed, developed, and delivered an e-mail–based communications transport technology used to deliver critical information between external customer systems and an internal software support lab. This technology has been patented. The project was exclusively engineered using C++ and design patterns. It spanned both BCUX and NT operating systems with a single source stream.

As **Senior Software Engineer,** I designed, developed, and delivered 100% of a cross-platform, completely reusable Object Oriented software library extensively used to track and monitor object lifetimes within C++ libraries. This library has been integrated into several customer products to provide "live" monitoring and tracking of software objects in released software which enables support labs to troubleshoot software in customer environments.

As **Senior Software Engineer,** I produced and delivered R&D lab-wide seminars to my peer group on the caveats and complexities of creating cross-platform code reuse libraries.

As **Senior Software Engineer,** I became a self-taught lab-wide expert on C++ and design patterns. **I obtained Microsoft Visual C++/MFC certification.**

Big Computer Company, Ft. Collins, CO, 1995–1998

As **Software Engineer,** I executed all phases of software development from initiation to CPE for multiple projects spanning languages including, Perl, C, C++, Pascal, AWK, LEX, YACC, Java, KSH and operating systems including BC-UX and NT.

OTHER WORK HISTORY

1994: <u>Test Engineer</u>, Sugarstream Systems, Hollywood Blvd., LA, CA
1990–94: <u>User Services Customer Consultant</u>, MST Computing Services, Mt. St. U., Bigsky, MT

EDUCATION/TRAINING

<u>B.S. Computer Science</u>, Montana State University, Bigsky, MT

Five most recent advanced education classes:
➢ Dynamic Leadership
➢ Attracting, Hiring, and Keeping Great People
➢ Technical Leadership
➢ Project Management Fundamentals
➢ Advanced Object Oriented Methods using C++
Language training:
➢ 3 Months German
➢ 3 Months Japanese
➢ 3 Years French

References and Salary History provided upon request.

*** 2005–Feb 2007 <u>Owned and operated</u> a franchise restaurant concurrent with my Big Computer Company responsibilities. During my nights, weekends, and holidays, I built, opened, and operated a franchise restaurant in downtown Ft. Collins. I took classes, read instructional documents, and met with consultants to gain enough knowledge to construct a business plan, which I submitted to a local bank to obtain financing for building and operating a new restaurant. Once financing was obtained, I worked with franchise corporate executives to locate and develop a location for our restaurant. Over the course of 8 months, I was the project manager who scheduled and coordinated architects, contractors, vendors, and franchise corporate members during construction of the restaurant. After screening and hiring the restaurant management and staff, I assured their training schedules were completed in time to meet all grand opening deadlines. Following a successful grand opening, I worked with management and staff daily on all facets of restaurant operations from scheduling to ordering to customer service to payroll and finances. In February of 2007, I negotiated the sale and transfer of ownership of this restaurant to new owners.

Aim for a Resume That's "Just Right" for the Situation

Considering the "Too Small," "Too Big," and "Just Right" descriptions you just read, in which category does your resume fall? As you work toward building documents that are "Just Right," keep the following analogy in mind.

In your lifetime, you've acquired a broad set of skills and knowledge. Everything you've studied, achieved, and completed can be considered as elements in your "master closet" of experiences, containing *everything* you've learned and lived through. Each item in this master closet is important to you and may be useful to your career success at some point in the future.

However, when you present yourself as a candidate for a specific career opportunity, including *every* item in your master closet of experiences doesn't make sense. For one thing, it's too much information to cram into a resume. For another, you end up looking unfocused. Instead, you want to aim to select only the pieces from your master closet that will allow you to create the "Just Right" outfit for a particular opportunity.

The following chapters walk you through a clear, step-by-step process to help you choose those "Just Right" elements of your background and present them in powerful, results-generating resumes to fit all your future career needs.

Why It's Worth Doing

For just a few minutes, imagine that you're a hiring manager. You've determined that you need to find just the right person to fill a marketing manager opening in your company. You developed a job description, ran a job ad both online and in the local papers, and in the last two weeks you've received more than 100 resumes. You've been dreading the process of going through the resumes (it will be so much work!), but you've set aside a few hours this morning to tackle the task.

You begin the chore, picking the first resume off the pile. A cover letter introduces Carol, who says that she saw your ad in the *News-Times* newspaper. There are several other paragraphs in her letter, but for now you flip to her resume. The first thing you notice is that she worked as a bookkeeper in her last job. Bookkeeper? You're hiring a marketing manager. You spend a few more seconds scanning her resume but quickly become frustrated because you're not seeing the kind of background you're looking for. Annoyed, you plunk Carol's resume in a place on your desk that you've decided will be for rejects.

Then you pick up the next resume, thinking to yourself that maybe this task won't be so arduous after all. Heck, if you can scan a resume in just a few seconds and see that the person isn't right for the job, maybe reviewing the resumes won't take as long as you had worried! The next candidate is Jose. His cover letter includes some bullet points that describe his marketing background. So good so far, you think, and turn past the cover letter to the resume. Jose clearly states at the top of his resume that he's looking for a marketing manager position. You also notice that he's working as a marketing specialist at a company now and that his bachelor's degree in business administration included a minor in marketing. Whoo-hoo! you think; this guy looks worth considering. Jose's resume lands in the "Maybe" pile.

You continue working through the stack of resumes, and within less than an hour you've sorted them into two neat stacks of "No way!" and "Maybe." Your next activity will be to look through the "Maybe" pile again to find five candidates to call in for interviews.

This step turns out to be a little more difficult than the first cut. After you spend a minute or two on each of the 20 resumes in your "Maybe" pile, 10 of them look very strong. Yet you want to interview only five. So you decide you have to use tougher criteria to help you choose. You review those 10 again, this time looking for reasons to eliminate five. Hmmm, although June's background is impressive, she doesn't list any concrete accomplishments. Michaela does,

describing a customer database project she orchestrated that resulted in a mailing list that generated 20 percent more sales in a single
year. June gets moved to the "No way!" pile.

You decide to use accomplishments—or lack of them—to help you
weed out four other candidates. Within 10 minutes, you've narrowed
the list to six candidates whose resumes seem to describe individuals
with backgrounds that look just right. You wanted five, but six is
workable. Whew! you think. Got through that part! Now on to the
next phase in the hiring process....

As you can see from living in the shoes of a resume screener (if only
for a few minutes), a "Yes" or "No" decision can boil down to just a
few key pieces of information. And as a motivated job searcher, you
want to make sure your resume is "Just Right."

Career Champ Profile: Sam

Sam had had a successful career in sales and sales management.
Now he was aiming for his next challenging career position and had
been job searching for three months. Yet after responding to more
than 30 sales management postings, he hadn't received one call for
an interview. "I have so much to offer a company. Why can't they see
that?" I looked over his resume. It was one page, very sketchy, and
based on the Goldilocks criteria, fell into the "Too Small" category.
"Looking at your current resume, I'd guess that you don't really
enjoy your work and have had a ho-hum career so far. Is that true?"
"Oh no!" Sam replied. "I've loved my work and have had many,
many impressive accomplishments. If only they'd call me in for an
interview, I could tell them all about what I've done!"

I suggested that instead of waiting for an interview to share those
juicy details about his background, we include some highlights in his
resume to help build the resume screener's interest. "Does a resume
screener really want to read *lots* of details?" Sam asked me. "Well,
not *too* many details," I replied. "We want to share just enough." This
was the resume we created for Sam, which generated excellent
results.

Sam Powers   *Sales Management*
5705 Scenic Stream Drive, Claremont, CA 93282
(333)111-2222, spowers@email.com

R esults-driven, accomplished **Advertising Sales Manager** with a proven track record for building high-performing teams and achieving outstanding levels of success; possess a keen ability to motivate teams to close sales through priority setting, relationship building, and consultative sales training; possess exceptional communication abilities and a drive to succeed.

ACHIEVEMENTS & AWARDS

Management & Leadership Excellence:
➢ Awarded **"Retail Manager of the Year"** from among over 90 managers company-wide (The Californian).
➢ Awarded **"Manager of the Year"** (The Californian).
➢ Received **"President's Award for Outstanding Service"** (Homeowners' Association).
➢ Earned Four **Dale Carnegie Excellence Awards.**
➢ Appointed **Chair, Fort Maynard Chamber of Commerce,** Environmental Committee.

Sales Accomplishments:
➢ Attained **19% sales increase** 2005–2006, and **75% sales increase** 2006–2007 (SCBD).
➢ Supported **25% increase** in ROP growth in 2007 (SCBD).
➢ Earned **"Rookie of the Year"** 2005 (SCBD).

WORK EXPERIENCE

Outside Sales / Special Projects Manager, Southern California Business Daily, 2005–Present
Sell and service accounts generating $400K in annual revenue for regional business news publication.
• Consistently increase sales through new account development and cultivation of existing accounts.
  ✓ **Increased sales by 75% in one year, and regularly attain or exceed sales quotas.**
• Propose and execute special events and publications to increase profitability, client exposure, and business opportunities. *Examples*: Green Summit, Morris Motors 75th Anniversary.

Classified / Retail Advertising Sales Manager, The Californian, 1998–2005
Provided team leadership to retail and classified advertising departments for daily newspaper.
• **Managed sales teams of 25+ members responsible for generating $13 million in annual revenues,** and achievement of sales targets 8 of 11 years.
  ✓ **Received nationwide and local awards for management excellence.**
• Designed and implemented comprehensive new-hire sales training, and reorganized department into more effective team approach:
  ✓ **Achieved higher-than-industry-average employee loyalty** through encouragement, praise, mentoring, and appropriate discipline.
• Possess a proven track record for successful management of budgets and expenses.
• Launched numerous profitable specialized publications by partnering with area organizations and supporters, and following projects through to successful completion.

EDUCATION & TRAINING

• University of Nebraska, English
• Skill development courses: **Dale Carnegie, American Press Institute,** and **Disney Institute**

Figure 2.3: Sam's resume.

Core Courage Concept

You may have been creating your resume the same way for years. Now, based on what you've just learned in this chapter, you may have discovered that your current resume approach is "Too Small" or "Too Big"...and now you need to make it "Just Right." Taking this step can seem scary. "Is it worth the risk to try a different way?" you may be worrying. "What if this approach turns out worse?" Although attempting something new *can* be scary, new approaches can help you achieve better results. As you move forward in this book, keep in mind that you can *always* go back to doing things as you did them before. Yet until you learn and try something new, you won't know which way works better for you.

Confidence Checklist

☐ Determine your current resume style.

☐ Aim for a resume that's "Just Right" for the situation.

Chapter 3

Create Your "Master Closet" of Experiences

As you learned in the preceding chapter, your aim is to create a resume that's "Just Right" for the career opportunity you're seeking. To do this, you want to be able to evaluate your full range of educational, life, and work experiences, and select exactly the right pieces of information to include. In this chapter, you record details for your Master Closet of experiences so that you'll have a wide range of information from which to choose.

Risk It or Run From It?

- **Risk Rating:** Easy sneezy. It's like taking an inventory of your closet.

- **Payoff Potential:** Great! You'll be reminded of (and most likely pleasantly surprised at) all the great tools and experiences you've acquired in your life so far.

- **Time to Complete:** An hour or less.

- **Bailout Strategy:** You can skip this chapter if you're comfortable with recalling pieces of your background as needed to support each step in the resume process.

(continued)

(continued)

- **The "20 Percent Extra" Edge:** Having a detailed record of your school, volunteer, work, and self-learning experiences makes it easy for you to quickly access relevant experience for a variety of purposes: resumes, interviews, cover letters, portfolios, and so on.

- **"Go for It!" Bonus Activity:** Read through any career and school records available to you, such as status reports, performance reviews, school transcripts, or scheduling calendars, to help remind yourself of experiences you may have forgotten.

How to Build a Comprehensive Experiences Inventory

While you may not believe it as this moment, you've done *a lot* of things in your life. And pretty much anything you've ever attempted, learned, and experienced may come in handy as you create your resume. For this reason, it's useful to review and document all the pieces of your background so that you have potential content for your resumes.

One way to look at this step in the process is that you're taking an inventory of everything you own in your "experience wardrobe." For instance, you have a collection of pants, shirts, undies, socks, accessories, and so on in your closet, dresser, and maybe also in storage. You've been hanging on to all those items because at some point, every item in that wardrobe may be useful to you, depending on the occasion, right? Similarly, every item in your experience wardrobe may also come in handy, depending on the resume you need to write. So now you want to create a written inventory of all those items.

Collect Any Info Already Available

Chances are, you may already have much of your experience wardrobe documented. As a first step, pull together any of former versions of your resume or performance reviews from current and previous positions that you may have in your files.

Create a Rough Outline of Your Professional History to Date

Now make a sketchy outline of your school and work history. It doesn't matter in which order you write this outline. Some people like to begin from their most current position and work backward, whereas other people prefer to begin with high school and work forward from there. Here's mine as an example, working from high school forward:

- Graduated from Bennett Sr. High School in Salisbury, MD, 1980.

- While in high school, worked as a lifeguard at Canal Woods swim club, and also at Gino's and Friendly's restaurants.

- Completed my freshmen year in college at Randolph Macon Women's College in Lynchburg, VA, and then transferred to University of Tennessee in Knoxville. (Didn't work at all in Lynchburg; just went to school.)

- Worked in the cafeteria at UT and also landed a job as a specialist in the complaint department for the 1988 World's Fair. Also had a job working as a graphic artist for a printer (can't remember the name of the place) and selling ads for the UT newspaper.

- Graduated from UT with a degree in communications in 1984 and moved to NH.

- Landed a job as a copywriter with First Software, a software distribution company in MA. Worked there for about three years.

- Got a job with Raster Technologies as a marketing communications specialist. Worked there for a few years.

- Took the same kind of job with Numerix. Worked there for about two years, and then the company was acquired by Alliant Computers. Then Alliant Computers was acquired by Mercury Computer Systems, and I was promoted to Marketing Communications Manager.

- Worked there for about three years and decided I wanted to make a career change.

- Left my job in marketing and went to graduate school at Colorado State University to earn my master's degree in career counseling.

- While in school, worked as a research assistant for Dr. Judy Whichard on a project for the Poudre Transition Center. Also held a part-time job as a copywriter for the housing department at CSU.

- Finished my master's degree in 1993 and tried to start my own business presenting workshops on how to make career changes. It failed quickly.

- Went to work for Bernard Haldane Associates as a career advisor. Worked there for three years.

- Opened my own career counseling practice in 1998. Have been doing the same work ever since.

- Also volunteer at my children's schools, church, and local community organizations.

This top-level review of my professional experiences took me about 15 minutes to write. As you can see, I didn't include dates for all my experiences because right now I can't remember them (but if I needed to, I could go back and figure them out.) This first step is just a rough sketch of what I've been doing since high school.

Add More Details to Your Outline

Now, add some detail to your rough outline, listing important responsibilities and experiences, particularly for those situations that were especially important and meaningful to you. For instance, this slice of time in my past I had some significant things going on for myself:

- Landed a job as a copywriter with First Software, a software distribution company in MA. Worked there for about three years. *Worked for Lori F. and Jim C. Wrote copy for ads and promotional materials describing hundreds of different software packages. One of my favorite projects was a 12 Days of Christmas promotion that was very successful. Learned how to use a computer in this job, how to work with service vendors to develop marketing materials, to juggle a lot of projects at the same time. One time I won an Employee of the Month award from among about 100 employees.*

- Got a job with Raster Technologies as a marketing communications specialist. Worked there for a few years. *Worked for Kristi F. Did similar promotional writing work, plus learned how to put together trade shows. My boss was traveling often, so often I was called upon to fill in for higher level things. I did well, and through the grapevine another company heard about me and offered me a job.*

With this step, you can get as detailed as you want. You may want to jot down every responsibility you can recall, along with significant projects and accomplishments. Or, like me, you may just want to write a few sentences.

Panic Point! Career Cowards often worry that they won't be able to recall something significant that might need to be included in a resume. If this sounds like you, take a deep breath and relax. At this stage in the process, it's okay if you can't remember all the details. Chances are, you haven't thought about some of these things for a long time! As you work through your resume development process, other details may come to you. But for now, not being able to recall all the details isn't a big deal...I promise!

For those details you can recall, you may want to include

- Specific job responsibilities

- Noteworthy projects you handled

- Promotions, degrees, certificates, and awards you received

- Classes or training programs you took that you particularly enjoyed and did well with

- Achievements or results especially important to you or to your employer

- Technologies and processes you learned

- People you worked for

That's it! You've created your master experiences inventory! (Wasn't too tough, was it?) Keep it handy because you may need to refer to it throughout your resume-development process.

Why It's Worth Doing

Going about your busy life, you can easily forget many of the things you've lived through. Yet those experiences may turn out to be valuable, especially as you work toward creating a resume that presents you effectively toward your next career goal.

Taking a few minutes to mentally walk down the path your life has taken allows you to recall and make note of important events and situations. Then, as you move through the process of developing your resume, you can look back on key points in your life and select the pieces of your background that are most relevant and that position you in the most effective way.

Taking a master experiences inventory is a simple step that can provide big resume rewards down the line!

Career Champ Profile: Jim

After seven years in the insurance industry, Jim wanted to get back into a job in accounting. "But I've been out of it for so long," he worried out loud to me. "Won't an employer think that all I can do is sell insurance, because that's what I've been doing for the last several years?"

To help calm his fears and move him toward creating an effective resume, I asked Jim to write his master experiences inventory, listing major positions, responsibilities, training, and accomplishments. Fifteen minutes later, he pushed his list across the desk to me and used his pencil to point at a section on the paper. "This right here is where I was doing most of my accounting work, and I loved it. That's what I want to do again." Using that information, we were able to create the following resume for Jim. It quickly resulted in several job interviews for accounting positions, moving him toward his career goal.

Core Courage Concept

When you think about landing the job you really want, it's likely that you also follow that thought with "Yeah, but am I really qualified for it?" Early in the resume development process, most of us (especially Career Cowards!) worry that we won't have enough of the "right stuff." Having a master inventory of all that you've done, learned, and accomplished at your fingertips can give you an instant confidence boost, as you review it and see that, yes, you do have what it takes!

James V. Smeed

2151 Aquamarine Lane
Fort Collins, CO 80521
(970) 555-6666 jsmeed77@hotmail.com

Assistant
Controller

Dedicated, Meticulous, Sincere

Experienced, accurate Assistant Controller / Accounting Manager with proven ability to successfully manage Accounts Payable, Accounts Receivable, and Payroll in a high-volume environment; organized, versatile professional skilled in collaborating with department managers on new projects and ongoing activities; strengths in creating and monitoring efficient, accurate accounting processes; track record for working collaboratively with Controller / Comptroller; possess strengths in supervising productive and loyal teams.

Work History

- ➤ *Recently relocated to Colorado; desire to return to* **Accounting** *profession.*
- ➤ **Agent / Owner,** GoodHands Insurance / Canyon Insurance, 2001–2008
- ➤ **Accounting Manager,** Cattle Services, Inc., 1992–2001

Accounting Expertise...
- Handled day-to-day accounting transactions (A/P, A/R, payroll) for feedlot operation with $50 million in annual sales.
- Reduced twice-monthly billing cycle turnaround from 2½ days to one day:
  - ✓ Developed and followed an efficient system of checks and balances to ensure accurate posting of daily activity and streamline processing time.
  - ✓ Improved throughput capability of the organization, supporting steady business growth.
  - ✓ Minimized billing-cycle time, allowing smoother overall operation of the company.
- Maintained an outstanding record for accounting accuracy and timeliness. Received frequent positive feedback from management for quality support to the organization.

Supervisory & Leadership Experience...
- Supervised accounting technician responsible for processing A/R, A/P, and payroll transactions.
- Cultivated loyal, productive results through compassionate, goal-focused leadership.
- Built strong interpersonal relationships with individuals throughout the company to facilitate smooth business operations.
- Demonstrated outstanding ability to diagnose and resolve problems with coworkers, customers, and employees.

Technical Competency..
- Successfully learned and used several software applications, including turnkey accounting software and insurance-industry programs.
- Possess strengths in identifying and implementing improvements in automation processes for greater efficiency and accuracy.

EDUCATION & LICENSES

- Bachelors Studies, Southwestern College
- Turnkey Computer Systems Accounting Software Training
- Property & Casualty Licensure, Colorado & Nebraska

Figure 3.1: Jim's resume.

Confidence Checklist

☐ Collect any information already available.

☐ Create a rough outline of your professional history to date.

☐ Add more details to your outline.

Chapter 4

Focus Your Resume for Success

reating your "Master Closet" inventory was energizing, wasn't it? Now you're even more motivated to create a Just-Right Resume that will excite decision makers and generate job interviews. Now you'll take the next step toward achieving that goal: deciding on your first career target and building the foundation of your successful resume.

Risk It or Run From It?

- **Risk Rating:** This step is a tiny bit risky. I'm going to ask you to choose a specific career target, and that makes some people squirm.

- **Payoff Potential:** Really, really big. The simple act of choosing a career target sets the stage for creating a resume that gets much better results.

- **Time to Complete:** 1 to 30 minutes (or a few months, if you need to do some career exploration first…).

- **Bailout Strategy:** Well, if you already know exactly the kind of position you're targeting and have sample job descriptions for that type of work, move on to the next chapter!

(continued)

(continued)

- **The "20 Percent Extra" Edge:** When you launch your resume toward a specific focus, you greatly increase your chances of actually achieving your goal. As few as five percent of job searchers truly define a career target for their resume. After you've completed this step, you'll be in the top five percent!

- **"Go for It!" Bonus Activity:** If you're aiming for more than one type of position, complete the recommended steps in this chapter for each of your career targets. Although this activity will take some extra time now, it will save you time later.

How to Focus Your Resume to Achieve Awesome Results

To build your resume on a solid foundation, you'll need to choose a career target. This concept may feel a little uncomfortable at first, yet I strongly urge you to hang in there to see how the process develops. The significant boost in results you'll receive from choosing a clear target should be enough to convince you!

Decide on Your First Resume Target

What kind of position are you aiming for? This is a big question. In fact, your answer to this single question will drive every step you take toward creating an effective resume, so it's important to choose a career target that fits for you. If you can say, "I'm looking for a position as an *X*" (for example, Webmaster), you're in good shape. If you can also define specific industries that are a good fit for you (such as "Webmaster in High-Tech Manufacturing or Medical Services"), even better!

Buuuuuuuut, what if you're not that clear about the kind of work you're aiming for? Or what if there are lots of jobs you'd be happy with, and you want your resume to present you effectively to a variety of positions? If either of these statements sounds like you, you're actually in the majority of job seekers. Yet from a resume standpoint, it's not a good majority to be in. Why? Because as we've already discussed, you have only a few seconds to get the resume screener's attention, and it's nearly impossible for a resume without a clear focus to communicate key aspects of your background quickly.

I realize that at this point in the process, you may not buy into my philosophy about the importance of choosing a career target for your resume. Fair enough. Yet ask yourself, "How effective have I been with my own approach to resumes?" If your resume is resulting in very few calls for interviews, you may want to consider trying my strategy. Choosing a clear career target and building your resume around that focus can help you create resumes that result in interviews 50 percent or more of the time.

Weigh "General" Against "Specific"

Job seekers frequently say to me, "I want to keep my resume more general so that I can use it for a lot of different opportunities."

After observing the job search results of literally thousands of job searchers, however, I've discovered that when it comes to resumes, the general approach just doesn't work very well. As the saying goes, when all you have in your toolbox is a hammer, every opportunity looks like a nail. But a hammer simply isn't the best tool for every opportunity. In fact, if you use a hammer for some jobs, you'll ruin the result.

Sticking with this analogy, sometimes you need pliers or a level. Ideally, you want to choose the tool that best fits the need. That's why a specific, customized resume is so important.

Panic Point! Career Cowards often fret that creating a custom resume for *every* opportunity will take tons of time and effort, and that they don't have the time, interest, and maybe ability to do that! They'd rather just get one good resume done and call it quits. Although the thought of creating customized resumes for *every* opportunity can seem overwhelming, keep in mind that we're going to take this process one baby step at a time, leading to a

(continued)

(continued)

> dynamite resume that delivers excellent results for you. Then, when you've learned the process, you'll see that creating customized, effective resumes can actually take very little time at all.

In fact, I once wrote several customized resumes for a single client. He had hired me to develop them for him because he'd been in a car accident, and his head injury made it difficult for him to write. So over the period of a few months, I developed about 5 to 10 customized resumes for him each week. After a week or so, I was spending less than five minutes to customize a resume for each opportunity. You read right: *less than five minutes.* When you learn the process, the pieces fall into place easily. And best of all, my client was landing a ton of interviews. On average, he would receive a call for an interview for about 50 percent of the jobs he applied to. Seeing that a 10 percent rate is average, he was thrilled with the result.

So even though thinking about choosing and developing a resume for a single career target may make you squirm a little, pick one for now so that we can move to the next step. Ideally, your target will clearly state a role, such as Marketing Manager, Accountant, Customer Service Representative, Quality Specialist, or Engineer. It may also clearly state an industry, such as Publishing, Antiques, or Real Estate. Both of these pieces are important, but the role is especially so.

Use Strategies to Identify the Right Career Target for You

Not sure which role to choose? Here are some ideas for defining a career role target for this first resume:

- **Use the title for a specific job to which you want to apply.** This is the easiest approach. Just rip the title right off the job description!

- **Consider the roles you've held before.** Were you a Sales Rep? Manufacturing Assembler? General Manager? If you've liked your former work, stick with one of those job titles as your career role target.

- **Bump yourself up a level.** If you've liked your former work but are looking for more of a challenge, consider aiming up one level higher. For example, if you've worked as an Accountant, maybe you want to aim for Accounting Manager or Controller. If being a Customer Service Rep was okay, but now you want more, consider the next step in that career path. It may be managing a team of reps or moving into a more technical aspect of that work, such as defining customer service processes. For clues, think about people who are involved in work that's related to yours and who are doing things that seem more interesting to you. What is their specific career role?

- **Poke around on a job search site for ideas.** Simply log on to a job search site, plug in the types of activities you like to do, and let the search engine do the work.

  For instance, when I logged on to www.monster.com and typed in **Solving Problems, Helping Customers, and Improving Processes**, it brought up job titles such as Customer Solutions Advocate, Report Writer, and Call Center Business Analyst (along with 5,000 other titles!) If you can find just a few titles and job descriptions that are appealing to you, that can help you choose a career role target for your resume.

- **Spend more time defining a career role *before* you write your resume.** Okay, this may not be the answer you were hoping for, but if you're really struggling with stating a career target, it may make sense for you to go back one step to first define the kind of work you want to do. Yes, going back will delay your resume-writing process for a while, but ultimately it can save you years of wasted time in a career fit that's wrong for you. An excellent resource for defining a career target is *The Career*

Coward's Guide to Changing Careers by yours truly. Defining your career role target can be a fun, energizing process that delivers life-changing results!

Make Your Resume Target Even More Effective by Also Choosing Some Industries

If you've defined your career role, you can make your resume even stronger by also deciding on some industries to target. For instance, if your career role is Project Manager, which industries are the best fit for your background and interests? As you would expect, managing projects in the landscaping industry is very different from managing projects in the teleservices industry. If you're able to choose some specific industries—as well as specific career role targets—your resume will be even stronger.

Why? Because if you know which industries you're targeting, you can tailor your resume with buzzwords and phrasing that are specific to that segment of the work world, and that will make your resume even *more* effective! For example, when I look at job descriptions for Project Manager in Landscaping, I find this type of terminology:

- Three to five years of landscape experience required

- Knowledge of water features, concrete, plant materials

- Ability to schedule labor and material deliveries of assigned projects

Now compare this to the phrasing I find for Project Manager in Teleservices:

- Background in developing and implementing both inbound and outbound telemarketing programs

- Ability to create teleservices scripts and call flows that meet program objectives

- Background in writing, implementing, and ensuring adherence to standard operating procedures

Pretty different, huh? And as you'll learn more about in the next chapter, the right keywords can make a huge difference in the results your resume generates. So, if at all possible, define your career target even further by also choosing some specific industries. A simple way to choose industries is to look through the yellow pages in the phone book. Flip through all the category headings and make a list of the industries that look appealing to you.

> **Note:** This technique has a double bonus: When you choose industry categories, not only do you improve the effectiveness of your resume, but you also make it easier to identify and present yourself to potential employers. Whoo-hoo! This gives you an awesome competitive edge that you'll read more about in chapter 17.

Why It's Worth Doing

I once had an in-depth conversation about resumes with a recruiter who locates and places top-level executives. He told me that less than five percent of the candidates he talks to can clearly define the kind of work they're seeking. "Focus is the single biggest problem most people have when it comes to career advancement. They don't know what they want—or if they do, they have a tough time communicating it—so it's nearly impossible for others to help them get there."

This recruiter looks at about 200 resumes every workday, initially spending just a few seconds on each one, hoping to determine whether the candidate's background is a match for any of the positions he's trying to fill. If he doesn't find the kind of information he's looking for—a clear career target and evidence of the candidate's ability to succeed in that area—he will very quickly move on to the next resume waiting for his attention.

Your resume, whether it's viewed by a hiring manager, HR representative, or recruiter, will be going through the same breakneck speed, "Tell me what you want and show me what you've got" evaluation. If you want to produce resumes that get awesome results, choose a career target.

Career Champ Profile: Tami

Tami had left her last job a half a year ago. After devoting close to 10 years to supporting attorneys as a paralegal in a law office, she was ready for a different challenge. But over the past 6 months, she'd sent her resume to jobs she found in the paper and received no nibbles at all.

I looked at her resume and could pretty much guess why she wasn't getting good results. "May I give you some honest feedback?" I asked her. She nodded her head. "You've worked as a dog groomer, a paralegal, a fund-raiser in nonprofit organizations, and as a student support aide at a university. Your background seems to be all over the board."

She took a deep breath. "I thought that since my background was so diverse, it would show that I'm qualified for lots of different kinds of positions." I laughed. "You would think that, wouldn't you?" I said. "But it doesn't work that way. I've discovered after observing the successes and failures of thousands of job searchers that the more general and unfocused your resume is, the less effective it is. What kind of job would you really like to get?"

"I'd *love* to get a job as an administrative assistant in a nice little business office, but no lawyers this time. They're too high maintenance!" she said smiling. So I worked with Tami to revise her resume this way.

I talked with Tami two days later. "Any changes we need to make to your resume?" "Oh! I've already been using it. I submitted it to a job I saw in the paper on Monday, and I got a call on Tuesday. I have an interview tomorrow. Can you believe it? It's the first call for an interview I've gotten in six months. Focusing my resume toward a specific type of work made a huge difference!"

Tami Bladson   *Administrative Support*
151 Westwood Avenue
Ft. Collins, CO 80521
(970) 226-0000, tb1982@cs.com

Self-motivated, well-organized **Administrative Professional** with strengths in problem solving, multi-tasking, English / grammar, and customer support; adept at processing incoming and outgoing communications involving phone calls, mail, fax, and e-mails; offer proven strengths interacting with and supporting customers, suppliers, and employees; experienced in ordering and monitoring inventory for office supplies and equipment; background in maintaining calendars and coordinating meetings and travel; skilled in preparing business communications and correspondence, including transcribing dictation and composing and editing complex letters and documents; able to track projects through to successful completion; conscientious, efficient, and possess a strong work ethic.

.............................**PROFESSIONAL EXPERIENCE**...............................

Administrative Support, *Various Temporary Assignments*, 2007–present
- Successfully completed support assignments through local employment agencies.
- Additionally, volunteer with NCAP and Crossroads Safehouse.

Administrative Assistant, *Brown, Smith & Jones, P. C.,* 2005–2007
- Performed general office work including extensive tape transcription, word processing, and editing of correspondence, memorandum, and research documents.
- Used MS Excel, Outlook, Word, and Internet Explorer to complete assignments.
- Arranged meetings and appointments, tracked billing, and revamped filing system.
- Performed paralegal duties, including legal research regarding Public Trustee and Bankruptcy Court documents to support firm partner in Real Estate, Banking, and Contract Law.

Office Support / Grooming, *Cute Dog! & Happy Tails Grooming Shops,* 2000–2005
- Scheduled appointments, handled money, and provided customer support.
- Employed patience, imagination, firmness, quick thinking, and dexterity in bathing, drying, clipping, and scissoring a variety of dogs.

Administrative Assistant, *Crebs Commercial Real Estate Group, Inc.,* 1994–2000
- Provided administrative support to VP-level executives.
- Handled monthly and quarterly billings, tax deposits, payroll accounts, and monthly financial statements; tracked litigation costs and fees using Excel.
- Established file storage and retrieval inventory, and maintained law library.
- Prepared correspondence, pleadings, trial briefs, depositions, and trial notebooks.
- Coordinated travel arrangements and in-house seminars.
- Supervised and trained file clerk.

....**EDUCATION**...

- **BS, Criminal Justice,** *Metropolitan State College,* President's Honor Roll
- **AA, Secretarial Science,** *Colorado Northwestern Community College,* Honor Roll
- **Paralegal Certificate,** *Denver Paralegal Institute,* ABA approved General Practice

Figure 4.1: Tami's new resume.

Core Courage Concept

Choosing a career target for your resume can feel scary. What if you make the wrong choice? What if you miss out on an even better opportunity because you're aiming for something else? You're right; you may be missing out on other possibilities by choosing a specific career target for your resume. Yet ask yourself this: Are you seriously being considered for any jobs now anyway? Is your resume getting you as far as being interviewed? In the words of TV psychologist Dr. Phil, "How's this approach working for you?"

On the flip side, by choosing a career target for your resume, you *greatly* increase your chances for getting a response from a hiring manager. Then, if you don't like the job, you can pass on it. *But at least you'll have the chance to decide!* And if you discover that a particular career target isn't right for you, you can choose another!

Confidence Checklist

☐ Decide on your first resume target.

☐ Weigh "General" against "Specific."

☐ Use strategies to identify the right career target for you.

☐ Make your resume target even more effective by also choosing some industries.

Chapter 5

Find and Choose Keywords to Strengthen Your Resume

Wow, you've chosen a career target for your resume...GOOD FOR YOU! If you can reach it, you should pat yourself on your back because you've set yourself up to make the rest of your resume-building process fun and successful. Your next step will be to take the career target you've chosen and begin to build a solid foundation for your resume. Don't worry...if the last step seemed especially difficult for you, this one will feel like a piece of cake!

Risk It or Run From It?

- **Risk Rating:** This step is about a 2 on a 1 to 10 scale, with 1 being low. No sweat.

- **Payoff Potential:** Large! This is one of those high-payoff, low-stress activities.

- **Time to Complete:** 15 to 60 minutes, depending on how detailed you want to get.

(continued)

(continued)

> - **Bailout Strategy:** Find a sample resume—on the Internet or in a book of resumes geared to your specialty—and copy that block of keywords and phrases. But y'know, this step really isn't that hard, and doing it can help get you in the mindset for creating the rest of your fabulous resume, so why not give it a go?
>
> - **The "20 Percent Extra" Edge:** Developing a solid block of keywords and phrases related to your career target instantly sets the stage for your resume to succeed.
>
> - **"Go for It!" Bonus Activity:** Increase the success of your resume over time by experimenting with different keywords. Keep track of the results each resume version generates and modify the keywords in your resume to continue improving your results.

How to Build a Dynamite Keyword Block

Okay, so what exactly is this "keyword block" that I keep referring to? Keywords are words and phrases that the person who writes a job description uses to describe the requirements for a particular position. For instance, here's a sample job description:

> Office assistant needed for busy appliance repair business. Pleasant phone voice and excellent customer services skills required. Must be proficient in MS Office, including Word, Access, Excel, and PowerPoint.

The words "Pleasant phone voice," "excellent customer service skills," "proficient," "MS Office," "Word," "Access," "Excel," and "PowerPoint" in this description are especially important, because when resume screeners begin sorting through the many resumes they receive in response to an ad, they're going to be looking for evidence that candidates have expertise in these areas. These words and phrases are examples of keywords.

Because the resume sorting process may happen either electronically (where a computer program sifts through a database of resumes to locate those with the greatest number of keyword matches) or visually (when resume screeners read all the submitted resumes in hopes of finding the skills they seek), it's important for you to include the right keywords in your resume. All the keywords you decide to include in your resume can be combined into a section called the "keyword block." For you, the resume writer, the keyword block is a "gimme," because it's easy to produce and highly effective.

Locate Job Descriptions Relevant to Your Position Target

The first step toward building your keyword block is simple and fun. Your goal is to locate a few detailed job descriptions that describe the kind of position you're seeking. Here are some ideas for finding what you need:

- If you have a detailed job description already, such as a job ad that you want to develop a resume for, you can count that as one of your three to four descriptions.

- If you don't already have a detailed description, log on to a job search site, such as www.monster.com, and hunt for job ads that describe the kind of work you're aiming for. When you log on to www.monster.com, the site first asks you to plug in the job title or keywords for the type of position you're aiming for and click Search. (Don't worry about selecting a particular geographic area. Your goal is to locate *sample* job descriptions, not actual job ads to respond to.) A long list of job ads will pop up.

For instance, when I typed in the job title **Technical Writer**, these were some of the listings that popped up:

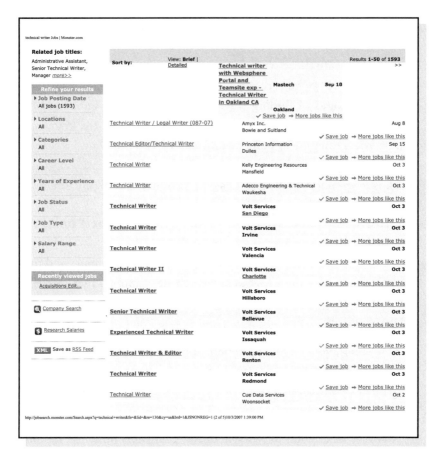

Figure 5.1: Search results for technical writer.

Working from the list that your search produces, begin clicking through to find ads that describe the kind of work you're aiming for. At this stage in the keyword-block-building process, it's better to find job descriptions with lots of detail rather than very concise ads so that you have more keywords to use.

- Another resource for keywords is www.americasjobbank2.com. This government site describes different career specialties. To locate potential keywords connected to your specialty, click a link in the Browse by Category section and follow the prompts.

As you locate position descriptions, copy the text and paste it into a word processing document. You'll wind up with a long list of job requirements that looks like this:

Description #1:

JDJ is looking for a Technical Writer to join our team in Westwood, NC. This writer will work with development engineers under the guidance of a senior technical writer to update context-sensitive online help, user guides, and release notes for state-of-the-art Data/IP communication test products. Work with developers and product marketing to create and maintain functional specifications. Work on projects across multiple locations creating customer documentation for communication test products including portable data analyzers as well as broad test systems including remote probes, test and monitoring OSS, and element management systems. Requirements: Quick learner, language and technology aptitude, personal initiative, degree in English or technical degree with demonstrated competence in technical writing. One to two years experience in technical writing field, best if in a data communications field. Must know RoboHelp, FrameMaker, Word. Nice to know: Graphics package such as Photoshop, Data/IP knowledge, configuration management tools/process.

Description #2:

CYNET is seeking an experienced Sr. Technical Writer to begin working on a project in Botbell, WA, ASAP! Document development work for three major projects; Complete technical system documentation, system and process flows based on business or functional requirements; work with information provided by developers; work with developers and analysts to obtain additional information; attend project meetings; technical report writing ability required; T-SQL and .NET; strong technical and communication skills; need someone to come in and hit the ground running with this project; any telecom-munications writing/technical experience helpful but not required.

Description #3:

Job Purpose: Prepares proposals by determining con-cept; gathering and formatting information; writing drafts; obtaining approvals. Duties: Determines proposal concept by identifying and clarifying opportunities and needs; studying requests for proposal (RFPs); attending strategy meetings. Meets proposal deadline by establish-ing priorities and target dates for information gathering, writing, review, and approval; entering and monitoring tracking data; coordinating requirements with contribu-tors; contributing proposal status information to review meetings; transmitting proposals. Gathers proposal information by identifying sources of information; coordi-nating submissions and collections; identifying and communicating risks associated with proposals. Develops proposal by assembling information including project nature, objectives/outcomes/deliverables, implementa-tion, methods, timetable, staffing, budget, standards of performance, and evaluation; writing, revising, and edit-ing drafts including executive summaries, conclusions, and organization credentials. Prepares presentation by evaluating text, graphics, and binding; coordinating printing. Maintains quality results by using templates; fol-lowing proposal-writing standards including readability, consistency, and tone; maintaining proposal support data-bases. Obtains approvals by reviewing proposal with key providers and project managers. Improves proposal-writing results by evaluating and redesigning processes, approach, coordination, and boilerplate; implementing changes. Updates job knowledge by participating in edu-cational opportunities; maintaining personal networks. Accomplishes organization goals by accepting ownership for accomplishing new and different requests; exploring opportunities to add value to job accomplishments. Skills/Qualifications: Presentation Skills, Written Communication, Graphic Design Skills, Technical Documentation, Layout Skills, Problem Solving, Deadline-Oriented, Process Improvement, Coordination, Strategic Planning, Market Knowledge.

Condense Your Long Keyword List to a Concise Keyword Block

Now that you've collected all this great keyword information, your next goal is to boil this long, long list of words into a concise keyword block. Follow this process to create an effective result:

1. Read through the text descriptions line by line and delete words or phrases that don't pertain to your background.

Panic Point! As you begin deleting phrases, be sure to delete them *only* if you truly have no experience at all with that particular skill. This is not the time to be modest about your background! If you've ever experienced a particular skill area *at all*, even if it was a single project or class, it counts.

2. Delete any company-specific information, such as where the description reads "CYNET is seeking an experienced Sr. Technical Writer to begin working a project in Botbell, WA, ASAP!"

3. Delete or combine any phrases that are similar. For instance, "work with developers and analysts to obtain additional information" and "work with information provided by developers" say pretty much the same thing, so you can combine them into one statement, "work with developers and analysts to obtain necessary information."

Now evaluate your keyword block. Ideally, you want to wind up with about 75 to 150 words. Is your keyword block still too long? Then continue with these steps:

1. Delete any phrases for aspects of the job that you consider to be of lesser importance. For instance, in my opinion, "work on projects across multiple locations" is assumed as something that most tech writers could do, so I cut it out.

2. Ask yourself again, "Can any of these requirements be combined because they're pretty similar?" Blend any phrases that can still be joined.

3. To reduce your keyword count further, consider including character descriptions—for example, "quick learner" and "self starter"—elsewhere in your resume, such as within work history descriptions.

4. If necessary, delete even more phrases that are of lesser importance, to reach your keyword-count goal.

This is what I came up with for the first cut at condensing my initial keyword block text:

> Work with engineers to update online help, user guides, and release notes; work with developers, analysts, and product marketing to obtain needed information and create functional specifications; knowledge of FrameMaker, Word, Photoshop; technical report and proposal writing experience; meet proposal deadlines by establishing priorities and target dates for information gathering, writing, review, and approval; develop technical documentation by working within objectives, timetables, staffing, budget, and standards of performance; maintain quality results by using templates; Presentation Skills, Written Communication, Graphic Design Skills, Technical Documentation, Layout Skills, Problem Solving, Deadline-Oriented, Process Improvement, Coordination, Strategic Planning, Market Knowledge.

Panic Point! "Oh no! I have too many words in my keyword block, and I don't feel as if I can delete any more of them. They're all important!" If this is happening to you, don't panic. Realize that you don't need to get rid of keywords *forever*. Instead, create a separate document labeled "Master Keywords List" to pull from in the future as you need to. As you create each resume, you can review your master keywords list and select only the keywords that pertain to a specific opportunity. Also, be kind to yourself regarding how you decide to include or delete information. There's no single "right" way to complete this step. Do your best, realizing that you can go back and make changes later if you need to. Resumes are a work in progress!

Decide How You Want Your Keyword Block Layout to Look

Now that you've created the core content for your keyword block, decide how you want it to look on your resume. Here are a few possible choices:

- List them as "Strengths" or "Expertise Areas." This approach is the easiest and doesn't require strong writing skills to execute. Simply create a section on your resume (I usually put it near the top, where it will be seen early on), title it "Strengths" (or the title of your choice), and then plunk in the keywords list you've just created:

  Strengths: Working with development engineers to update online help, user guides, and release notes; collaborating with developers, analysts, and product marketing to obtain needed information and create functional specifications; knowledge of FrameMaker, Word, Photoshop; technical report and proposal writing experience; meeting proposal deadlines by establishing priorities and target dates for information gathering, writing, review, and approval; develop technical documentation by working within objectives, timetables, staffing, budget, and standards of performance; maintaining quality results by using templates; Presentation Skills, Written Communication, Graphic Design Skills, Technical Documentation, Layout Skills, Problem Solving, Deadline-Oriented, Process Improvement, Coordination, Strategic Planning, Market Knowledge.

- Another option is to turn your keyword content into a paragraph describing you. With this method, you should make sentences out of the keywords so that the paragraph is readable and has a nice flow. You can do this by adding in lead phrases, such as

  - Offer expertise...

  - Experienced...

  - Proven track record in...

  - Adept...

  - Expert...

  - Strengths...

  - Knowledgeable...

  - Proficient...

  - Qualified...

  - Skilled...

  - Possess...

  - Able to...

  - Deliver...

...and so on. And a good way to get the paragraph started is to list your position target right up front. Here's an example:

Experienced, qualified **Technical Writer** adept at working with development engineers to update online help, user guides, and release notes; skilled in collaborating with developers, analysts, and product marketing to obtain needed information and create functional specifications; offer knowledge of FrameMaker, Word, and Photoshop; possess background in technical report and proposal writing; able to meet proposal deadlines by establishing priorities and target dates for information gathering, writing, review, and approval; proven track record for developing technical documentation by working within objectives, timetables, staffing, budget, and standards of performance; proficient in maintaining quality results by using templates; offer strengths in presentation skills, written communication, graphic design, layout, and problem solving.

- A third approach is to write a short lead-in statement, followed by keyword bullets. This works especially well when you want to highlight certain technical skills:

    Experienced, qualified **Technical Writer** with expertise in the following:

    - Working with development engineers to update online help, user guides, and release notes

    - Collaborating with developers, analysts, and product marketing to obtain needed information and create functional specifications

    - Knowledgeable in FrameMaker, Word, and Photoshop

    - Technical report and proposal writing

    - Meeting proposal deadlines by establishing priorities and target dates for information gathering, writing, review, and approval

    - Developing technical documentation by working within objectives, timetables, staffing, budget, and standards of performance

    - Maintaining quality results by using templates

Whichever approach you decide to try, keep in mind that there's no single right way to create a keyword block. You may end up using different approaches with different resumes, so view your first attempts as experiments until you hit upon a method that feels effective to you.

On a final note, you've probably noticed that I separate keyword phrases by semicolons. Grammatically, this is an incorrect use of semicolons (and I'm sure my editor had a fit not correcting the keyword block examples in this book!). However, in many cases your keyword phrases will not be written in complete sentences, and if you ended each phrase with a period, your word processing program would probably highlight the phrase as a fragment sentence, creating unsightly underlining in electronic versions of your resume. Bottom line, I use semicolons because they work nicely in a keyword block, even if my English teacher would debate my choice.

Create Your Resume Header and Insert the Keyword Block into Your Resume

Whoo-hoo! You're in the home stretch now. Open a word processing file and start building your resume by typing in your header information. Include the following data in your header:

- **Name:** Choose the name you prefer to be called. If your name is unusual, consider also including a small line underneath it providing clues about how it's pronounced.

- **Address:** It's important to show where you live (or will be living) to help hiring managers determine how accessible you are. Most positions will not provide relocation expenses, so if it all possible, show a local address. In some cases this will mean setting up a post-office box in the city where you plan to move and having your mail forwarded to you. A post-office box is relatively inexpensive, so it's a good investment if you're serious about finding work in a new location. A post-office box is also helpful if you don't want to give out your home address.

- **Phone number:** I recommend that you list only one phone number on your resume. Listing more than one can be confusing to resume screeners. "Which one should I call?" they may wonder. And if deciding which one to call takes too much effort, your resume may be passed over altogether. I recommend choosing a phone number with a clear, professional voice mail message on the other end—one that is not likely to be answered by your six-year-old daughter who will forget to let you know that Ms. Williams at ABC Company contacted you to set up an interview. It's also wise *not* to use your phone number at work. A hiring manager may worry about you also making inappropriate use of *his* resources if he took the risk of hiring you.

- **E-mail address:** I'm surprised how many people forget to include an e-mail address on their resume. E-mail (as you already know, I'm sure) has grown to be the most popular form of business communication. Many hiring coordinators will want to e-mail you if they're interested in arranging an interview, so if at all possible, include your e-mail address in your header. If you're worried about receiving lots of junk mail in your e-mail account, set up a separate account to list on your resume, and shut it down after you've completed your job search. (Oh, and choose an e-mail handle that doesn't position you unattractively, such as tightbuns@hotchick.com.)

- **Your career target:** Now that you've defined the position you're aiming for, you'll want to state it clearly in your header. This makes it easy for resume screeners to quickly determine the kind of position you're aiming for. (Remember…screeners may be sorting through hundreds of resumes, hiring for multiple positions, and you want them to know immediately what you're aiming for.) Keep in mind that you will change and customize the exact title of your career target, depending on the opportunity. For instance, one week you may respond to a job ad for a Sales Professional, so you would list that title on your resume. The next week, you may apply to a position opening for Business Development Specialist, so you would change the title in your header to reflect it. Here's a header example.

Lauren Toernihoj   *Event Coordinator*
(pronounced "turn-i-hoy")
P.O. Box 432
Cheyenne, WY 82001
(702) 238-5555, ltoernihoj@gmail.com

Figure 5.2: Header example.

After you've created your header, drop in your keyword block, and voilà, your resume is off to a brilliant start!

Panic Point! Worried about including personal information, such as your name and address in your resume? Then consider putting together a confidential resume. It's fine to list your initials only (rather than your full name), the region of the country where you live, a cell phone number (that can't be traced using address lookup services), and an unidentifiable e-mail.

Why It's Worth Doing

"That keyword block thing looks clunky. I'm not even sure I want to include one in my resume," you may be thinking. Okay, I'll agree with you that it looks a little weird, but bottom line, it can *greatly* improve the response you receive to your resume. It can be compared to adding Miracle-Gro to your plants. The improvement in results is phenomenal!

As you're putting together your resumes, it's important to continually remind yourself of the process it has to go through to get you the result you want. If you're responding to a job ad with your resume, chances are very good that it will either wind up in a stack of other hard-copy resumes (and it's not unusual for 100+ other resumes to be in that stack along with yours!) or in an electronic database (again, with hundreds of other resumes), awaiting the next step in the review process.

From there, the resume screener—often someone who is *not* the hiring manager—will then need to sort through those 100+ documents to choose a reasonable number of candidates to contact about an interview. This person, whether a human resources coordinator, a department administrator, or the hiring manager, will want to get through this sorting process as efficiently as possible. Believe me, resume screeners are *not* settled into a comfy easy chair, sipping tea, and reading through those resumes like they're devouring the latest great novel. No, they're looking through them quick, quick, quick, thinking, "Based on my initial evaluation" (usually about 10 seconds long), "does this person appear to have what I want?" If not, your resume gets dumped in the reject pile.

The keyword block, especially when positioned near the top of your resume, communicates to screeners almost immediately that you're on the correct playing field. Seeing words and phrases that relate to the screeners' priorities quickly builds confidence that you're probably worth an interview.

This keyword block is even more important if your resume is being screened electronically. In this case, human eyes aren't even looking at your resume during the first screening…*a computer program is sorting them*. And if the sorting program doesn't find certain keywords, you've missed your chance.

So even though the keyword block may look weird to you, at least consider giving it a try for a while. Send out a number of resumes with a keyword block included and see what kinds of results you get. You'll most likely be pleasantly surprised.

Career Champ Profile: Kim

Kim wanted to find a job as a patient admissions representative with a local hospital. Although she'd never held a patient admissions position before, she had succeeded in several customer service positions and had many skills that could be applied to patient admissions jobs. However, her existing resume painted a picture of her as a customer service representative for an international sales company.

One of the first steps Kim took toward creating an effective Patient Admissions resume was to locate three Patient Admissions job descriptions. The phrases used in those ads gave Kim the lingo and priorities she needed to present herself more convincingly as a patient admissions representative. She condensed her long list of phrases into a keyword block containing about 100 of the most important words and phrases and then built the rest of her resume to support her career goal.

When finished, her new resume clearly positioned her as a patient admissions rep, helping Kim land more interviews for the jobs she really wanted.

Core Courage Concept

Do you *truly* have what it will take to present yourself convincingly to a potential employer? Bottom line, that may be what you're asking yourself as you build a keyword block for your resume. If you're struggling with evaluating your own skills against those described in job ads, consider what you've been able to succeed with in other positions. Even if you had just a little experience in an area, were you able to learn more and ultimately handle the requirement effectively? As you develop keyword blocks for your resume, give yourself the benefit of the doubt. You know in your heart that you have great things to offer a potential employer. Create a meaty, effective keyword block to help decision makers realize that, too!

Kim Campbell   *Patient Admissions*
6439 Slider Court
Fort Collins, CO 80523
(970) 555-3131, kimcampbell@hotmail.com

E ffective, customer-focused bilingual (English / Spanish) Support Specialist with expertise in working one-on-one with individuals to determine needs, provide service, and solve problems; possess background in discussing finance and service options with customers, and following through to ensure timely, complete payment; adept at working with customers in high-stress situations to provide support and develop productive plans of action; possess proficiency in billing and collection processes; able to work well under pressure and handle sensitive information and multicultural matters; offer excellent interpersonal, communications, and organizational skills; proficient in MS Office, including Excel, Word, PowerPoint, and Outlook.

WORK HISTORY & RELATED EXPERIENCE

➤ **Bilingual Customer Support,** Hecht Company, 2001–Present
➤ **Teller,** First Regional Finance, 2001
➤ **Sales Associate,** Lovely Fine Jewelry, 1999–2000
➤ **Sales Associate,** Macy's, 1996–1999
  Additional experience in bookkeeping. Details on request.

Patient / Customer Support Expertise..
- Adept in customer-focused positions, assisting clients with financial and service matters. Consistently receive high ratings from management and customers for service excellence.
    - ✓ **Possess an outstanding ability to work within established procedural guidelines.**
- Offer language fluency in both English and Spanish:
    - ✓ **Worked daily with Spanish-speaking clients to successfully fulfill service requests.**
- Provide day-to-day written and verbal English / Spanish communication support to international customers, ensuring quality execution of contracts and services.

Bookkeeping & Medical Background..
- Experienced in processing high volume of financial data, including balancing cash drawers, processing transactions, preparing reports, and following through on collections matters.
    - ✓ **Financial processing performance has been consistently accurate and on time.**
    - ✓ Successfully collected 80% on past-due accounts through diligence and positive interactions with customers.
- Medical benefits knowledge includes intensive one-on-one training with benefits expert covering key procedural and information topics.

Technical & Teamwork Skills..
- Possess a proven track record as an effective team player:
    - ✓ **Currently work in fast-paced, high-stress environment, and consistently achieve high marks on performance reviews for ability to perform effectively in teams.**
- Highly skilled in computer applications including MS Word, Excel, Internet, and databases.

EDUCATION

- **B.A. International Spanish,** Minor in Business, University of Colorado, 2000

Figure 5.3: Kim's new resume.

Confidence Checklist

☐ Locate job descriptions relevant to your position target.

☐ Condense your long keyword list to a concise keyword block.

☐ Decide how you want your keyword block layout to look.

☐ Create your resume header and insert the keyword block into your resume!

Chapter 6

Prioritize and Select the Most Relevant Parts of Your Background

Already you've built a strong foundation for your resume's success, made up of a clear career target, a selection of results-producing keywords, and a focus on the top key skill areas. From here, you'll evaluate which parts of your background are most relevant and decide which of your experiences deserve prime positioning in your resume. This is a fun, energizing step in your resume-development process.

Risk It or Run From It?

- **Risk Rating:** Still pretty low. You're going to make some choices about what to include in your resume, and that might feel a tiny bit stressful. But keep in mind that resumes are a work in progress. You can always go back and select different pieces later.

- **Payoff Potential:** Way worth it. Making good choices at this step in the process will lead you to an excellent resume result.

- **Time to Complete:** 15 to 30 minutes.

(continued)

(continued)

- **Bailout Strategy:** Hmmm...I'm not sure that you can skip this part. At some point you'll need to choose which pieces of your background to include in your resume. If you want to postpone this step for now, jump to the next chapter, decide on your resume format, and then bounce back to complete this step.

- **The "20 Percent Extra" Edge:** You've been to social events where the best-dressed attendees get the most attention as well as primo perks. Putting together the right combination of elements in your resume will launch you into the realm of the "best-dressed" resumes.

- **"Go for It!" Bonus Activity:** If you want to take this activity to the next level, work with someone who knows you well to identify parts of your background that are especially relevant. Often, brainstorming with another person can help you come up with several more great ideas!

How to Decide Which Parts of Your Background to Include in Your Resume

In the next few steps, you're going to review your experience and background and decide which pieces make sense to include in the resume you're creating. This process will be very much like looking through your closet and deciding what to wear to a special event. Similarly, keep in mind that you have the option to consider several options and to discard them if they don't feel right. "I'm going to experiment with lots of ideas!" is an awesome attitude to have at this stage of writing your resume.

Choose the Most Important "Key Skill Areas" for Your Resume

As a first step to choosing key parts of your background, you'll need to decide which skill areas deserve top priority. This is especially important *because the key skill areas you select will make it easier to make decisions about content for your resume!* Because you've already decided on your career target, identifying the key skill areas should be relatively easy. Begin by pulling out the keyword block you created in chapter 5. Read through the terms and phrases and be on the lookout for the responsibilities that are most essential to success in the position.

For example, if I take this keyword block from chapter 5…

> Experienced, qualified **Technical Writer** adept at working with development engineers to update online help, user guides, and release notes; skilled in collaborating with developers, analysts, and product marketing to obtain needed information and create functional specifications; offer knowledge of FrameMaker, Word, and Photoshop; possess background in technical report and proposal writing; able to meet proposal deadlines by establishing priorities and target dates for information gathering, writing, review, and approval; proven track record for developing technical documentation by working within objectives, timetables, staffing, budget, and standards of performance; proficient in maintaining quality results by using templates; offer strengths in presentation skills, written communication, graphic design, layout, and problem solving.

…and read through it a few times, the skill areas that jump out most strongly for me are

- Working with others

- Technical writing

- Computer skills

- Project management

Although several skill areas are mentioned within the keyword block, these are what I would consider to be *the most important skills*. What are the most important skills within your keyword block?

If you're feeling unsure about which skills are most important for your career focus, make use of these resources to narrow your choices:

- **Log onto www.careeronestop.org and search for a description of your occupation.** At the top of the description is a list of key skill areas for each occupation. But there's a good chance that your occupation may not be listed on this Web site. The occupations that are included are those that the government considers to be the most popular occupations within the world of work today, yet only a few hundred of the tens of thousands of career specialties are included. So if yours isn't listed there, don't worry. One or more of the following steps will also help.

- **Ask some experts.** It's likely that you know a few specialists (teachers, managers, coworkers) who have worked in your career field for a while. Contact them and ask what they consider to be the most important skill areas to do your job well.

- **Trust your gut.** You probably have a pretty good idea about which skills are most important to the career target you've chosen, so select the top three to five based on your own expertise. For instance, in my work as a career counselor, I can say with confidence that the skill areas most key to my work are the ability to use effective counseling techniques with clients; a knowledge of career and industry information and trends; and strong communication skills for conversing with clients, writing resumes and materials, and presenting workshops.

In the following spaces, list the three to five skill areas most important to your career target:

1. _____

2. _____

3. _____

4. _____

5. _____

Panic Point! At this stage in the process, Career Cowards often feel paralyzed about which key skill areas to choose, worrying that they're not choosing the "right" ones. Or they may have more (maybe many more!) than five that they want to use. Is this you? If so, for now, it's fine to write down several possible key skill areas, even if it's a list of 20! As you work through the next step in this chapter, it's likely that your skills will begin to prioritize themselves into a list of the top three to five, or that you'll see how you can combine multiple skills into just a few categories.

Select Relevant Pieces of Your Background and Experience

Good for you...you've chosen some key skill areas to work with. Now you'll pick out pieces of your background to support these topics. This can be an energizing, confidence-building activity, so get ready to have some fun! To do this, pull out the master experiences inventory you created in chapter 3. (As a reminder, this is your "closet" of potential items to choose from.) Also have your key skill areas list handy.

Now, working through one key skill area at a time, ask yourself, "Which pieces of my background best support Key Skill Area #1?" Then read through your master experiences inventory, as well as any previous resumes, performance reviews, or other documents that will help you recall pieces of your background as they relate to that skill area.

As you work through this activity, be on the lookout for

- Times when you used that key skill area in work, volunteer, school, or personal experiences.

- Special projects, challenges, and accomplishments that especially demonstrated your use with that skill.

- Documented "proof" of your expertise with this skill. This proof might include certificates, degrees, comments on performance reviews, or letters of appreciation from others.

Please keep in mind that you don't need data from *every* area I've identified here; these are just ideas for where you might gather information. As you come up with pieces of evidence to back up your expertise in a particular skill area, note them in a list. Ideally, you will want to identify at least three pieces of evidence for every key skill area.

Panic Point! Struggling to find proof of your background with a particular skill area? Deep down, Career Cowards worry that they won't stack up. Fretting that you're not "good enough" is pretty normal. Helping thousands of people write their resumes, I've discovered that most people experience an "I don't have enough to offer!" panic attack as they begin this step. However, I've also seen that if they push through their initial fear, ideas begin to flow more easily, and soon they discover that they *do* have some evidence, even if it's just a few points. Sometimes it helps to set aside a key skill area that's causing you anxiety and to come back to it later.

You may also discover that you have *hundreds* of pieces of evidence for a particular skill area. Lucky you! If this is the case, jot down several instances, aiming to list those that are the most significant.

When she was brainstorming content for her resume (shown in the "Career Champ Profile" section of this chapter), Bronwyn identified these three key skill areas in line with her goal to land a Title Clerk/Closing Assistant position:

1. Customer service expertise

2. Knowledge of the real estate industry

3. Administrative support skills

She was then able to think of a few specific examples from her background to create this list of experiences for one of those skills, gathering evidence from many different times in her life:

Key Skill Area #1: Customer Service Expertise

- Owned my own jewelry-making business for several years. I provided lots of support to customers during this time.

- Worked for Nordstrom as a customer service clerk, and Nordstrom is rated one of the top companies in customer service in the world, so I got great customer service training there.

- Received letters from many happy customers for excellent service provided.

- Provided customer support to clients while working at the insurance company.

Create Additional Lists of Evidence for Your Other Key Skill Areas

Now that you've developed a list for your first key skill area, move on to the next, and the next, until you've developed a listing for all of them. Here are a few suggestions as you complete the rest of this activity:

- It's okay to list a piece of experience in more than one key skill category. For instance, in addition to helping customers at the insurance agency, Bronwyn could also list other things she did in that job to support her additional key skill areas, including completing homeowners' documents for her Real Estate Knowledge section and handling numerous office duties for the Administrative key skill area.

- As you review your past, make note of any specific projects and achievements you recall. These accomplishments can be highlighted on your resume to help you stand out from the competition.

- At this point, don't worry about which pieces of information you'll ultimately choose to include in your resume. For now, you're just brainstorming ideas.

When you've finished brainstorming lists for each key skill area, congratulate yourself. You've just completed a *very* important step in your resume development process!

Why It's Worth Doing

As they write their resumes, many people fall into the trap of including lots of information about their background that aren't relevant to the career target they're pursuing. This can be a big problem because resumes with too many extraneous details typically wind up in the "No thank you!" pile, and the job searcher winds up with poor results.

By taking the time at the start of your resume-creation process to identify the skill areas that are most important to the resume screener—as well as to select pieces of your background that are particularly relevant—you go a long way toward setting yourself up to achieve higher levels of success. Plus, there's an additional bonus to identifying and focusing on key skill areas: It makes writing a great resume so much easier!

Career Champ Profile: Bronwyn

Bronwyn had decided to target title clerk/closing assistant positions with her resume, even though she had never actually held that type of position before. Her background was broad, including working as a self-employed artist for many years; as a customer service clerk with a major department store; as an entrepreneur, buying, renovating, and selling homes; and as an office clerk within the insurance industry. In line with her goal to land a title clerk/closing assistant position, she decided that these three key skill areas were most important:

1. Customer service expertise

2. Knowledge of the real estate industry

3. Administrative support skills

Looking through her four pages of notes from her master experiences inventory, Bronwyn at first panicked that she didn't have enough real estate industry knowledge. "How about when you were buying, renovating, and selling houses?" I prompted her. "Did you have to work with any real estate documents then?" "Oh, sure!" she said, her face brightening. "I'd forgotten all about those. Plus, I just remembered that years ago I studied for and passed the real estate licensing exam in Oregon. I guess I do have some useful real estate knowledge to offer!"

Bronwyn continued making lists of her relevant experience related to her key skill areas, ultimately creating a wonderful list of relevant background, and we were able to create this resume for her.

Core Courage Concept

Do all these steps seem like a lot of work just to create a resume? You're right! Yet keep in mind that in addition to building your improved resume, you're also learning a new process, and that takes a lot of time and energy! With each step forward, you are moving yourself closer to achieving your goal of developing a rewarding career. Although these steps may cause you to sweat a little, it's worth the effort. In the end, you'll be so pleased with the result that your risks and effort will generate for you.

Bronwyn O'Shay

316 Laclaine Road
Delray, CO 80335
(303) 442-4775, bronwyn111@gmail.com

Title Clerk–
Closing Assistant

Accurate, customer-focused **Real Estate Support Specialist** with proven skills in maintaining relationships with clients to ensure satisfaction and loyalty; offer proven abilities in gathering property data, entering it accurately into computer programs, and meeting established deadlines; able to set up and maintain organized, accurate real-estate files; adept at establishing priorities, managing multiple projects, and meeting deadlines; possess strengths in working with others to ensure a timely, successful result; skilled in e-mail, MS Word, and Internet; personable and professional.

WORK HISTORY & RELATED EXPERIENCE

- ➤ **Customer Service / Sales,** *Nordstrom,* 2006–2007
- ➤ **Real Estate Student / Broker,** *Exit Realty Group,* 2005–2006
- ➤ **Real Estate Remodeling,** *Various Projects,* 1993–2004
- ➤ **Jewelry Design & Sales,** *Part-Time Positions,* 10+ years of experience
  Additional experience in Insurance & Teaching—details provided on request

Real Estate Industry Knowledge..

- Successfully studied for and completed real estate broker licensing exam.
- Possess knowledge of real estate documentation for sale and purchase agreements.
- Gathered required data for the purchase and sale of numerous properties, and successfully entered information into appropriate documents and files. *Example*:
  - ✓ Oversaw preparation of accurate and complete real estate documentation for purchase, renovation, and sale of numerous real estate properties.
- Provided support for real estate office activities and open-house events.

Customer Service Expertise...

- Worked for leading customer service organization (ranked #4 nationally), serving clients with outstanding support and problem solving.
- Built successful relationships with customers and ensured long-term loyalty by meeting customer needs in a timely, quality manner.
- Able to work both independently and as part of a team to complete projects on time.

Administrative Support...

- Prepared insurance policies and delivered on time to support real estate escrow closings.
- Maintained detailed, accurate real estate property data to support the successful sale and purchase of numerous properties.
- Skilled in computer programs including MS Office applications and Internet; able to learn and apply new programs quickly and effectively.

EDUCATION & LICENSES

- Passed Real Estate License exam in Oregon
- BFA, Colorado State University, cum laude

Figure 6.1: Bronwyn's new resume.

Confidence Checklist

☐ Choose the most important "key skill areas" for your resume.

☐ Select relevant pieces of your background and experience.

☐ Create additional lists of evidence for your other key skill areas.

Part 2

Write and Format Your Resume

Chapter 7

Scope Out Your Work History Section

You're well on your way toward creating a strong resume that generates excellent results for you. You've decided on your career focus, identified the key skill areas for your target, and gathered concrete evidence of what you have to offer relevant to the decision maker's priorities. Now you'll combine the effective resume strategies you've learned so far to create a strong Work History section.

Risk It or Run From It?

- **Risk Rating:** Relatively slight. Although this section is very important, putting it together using the guidelines in this chapter will allow you to handle it brilliantly.

- **Payoff Potential:** Successfully execute the Work History section in your resume, and you'll open many more career doors for yourself.

- **Time to Complete:** 15 to 30 minutes.

(continued)

(continued)

- **Bailout Strategy:** Because this is an essential section in your resume, you're going to need to get it done somehow, sometime. You could jump to another chapter for now and come back later. Or you could talk someone into creating it for you.

- **The "20 Percent Extra" Edge:** Most job searchers don't put much thought into how they're presenting their work history; they just mindlessly list job titles, employer names, and time frames. By being more strategic about how and what you present, you can position yourself more successfully with very little effort.

- **"Go for It!" Bonus Activity:** After you've created your outline, show it to a few people and ask them to describe what they perceive your work history to be. Sometimes we're not able to see the "forest for the trees," and hearing others' opinions can help us identify ways to improve our results.

How to Create Lists of Your Work History Components

Your aim with this section of your resume is to convey the following to the resume screener:

- You appear to be a reasonably stable person.

- You don't appear to be too old and expensive (and in some cases, too young).

- You've done work in the past that somehow relates to the position to which you're applying.

Depending on your personal situation, accomplishing these objectives may seem like a tall order. However, one or more of the following work history presentation techniques will provide you with an effective strategy.

As a first step, pull out the experiences inventory you created in chapter 3, as well as the objective you chose in chapter 4, and the key skill areas you defined in chapter 5. These items will help you make wise choices and keep you on track.

Now make some notes about your basic work history information. We'll be coming back to tweak this info eventually, so don't worry about making it "perfect" right now. Fill in the following, keeping in mind that internships, school, contributions at home, and volunteer efforts can all qualify as *work* and therefore can be considered as inclusions within this section:

Most Recent Job Title	Name of Employer	Year(s) Worked
Next Most Recent Job Title	Name of Employer	Year(s) Worked
Next Most Recent Job Title	Name of Employer	Year(s) Worked

Continue filling in the list of jobs as far back as you can remember.

Also write down this information:

Most Recent Training	Name of Institution	Year(s) Attended
Next Most Recent Training	Name of Institution	Year(s) Attended
Next Most Recent Training	Name of Institution	Year(s) Attended

List all your education and training. Again, we'll decide later which pieces to use.

Now list any volunteer experiences:

Most Recent Volunteer Role	Name of Institution	Year(s) Worked
Next Most Recent Volunteer Role	Name of Institution	Year(s) Worked
Next Most Recent Volunteer Role	Name of Institution	Year(s) Worked

Finally, list anything else that has taken a big chunk of your adult life in a productive way. For instance, you may have spent time as an at-home parent, caregiver for a family member, or coordinator for a home improvement project:

Role You Served	Type of Project	Year(s) Worked
Other Role You Served	Type of Project	Year(s) Worked

Consider Options for How to Present Your Information

Going forward, I want you to think of all the information you've just listed as pieces to a puzzle, and your mission is to put these pieces together to create a work history picture that will be appealing to resume screeners. Your goals for this step should be

- To show 5 to 15 years of responsible activity

- To avoid looking too "hoppy" by listing too many short-term positions

- To account for any major timeline gaps

- As much as possible, to relate your experiences to your current career target

Panic Point! Older Career Cowards frequently wrestle with how much of their work history to include. "Fifteen years of work history…I have many more than that! Don't they count?" they often wonder. The answer is, "Maybe yes…maybe no." Keep in mind that your goal with your resume is to communicate key pieces of your background while also getting the resume screener excited to interview you. If you present more than 15 years of experience, *you run the risk of looking too old and/or expensive on paper.* While you may choose to present pieces of information from earlier work experiences somewhere in your resume, you probably *don't* want to list work history dates that go back more than 15 years.

In this chapter, you're going to focus on how you'll organize your job title or function, the names of the organizations where you've worked, and the years spent with each assignment. Later, depending on the format you choose for your resume (discussed in chapter 10), you may decide to go back and include specific details about your job responsibilities as well. I promise we'll cover this part later in the book, but for now, concentrate only on the job title or function, name of the organization, and dates.

Another comment about dates: You'll see in these examples that we show years only, rather than months and years. I strongly prefer this method for the following reasons:

- Showing years only, rather than months and years, looks "cleaner" on a resume, allowing you to include fewer details to distract resume screeners from the really important information.

- Listing years only also provides you greater flexibility for showing a cohesive work history. For instance, if you left one job in September 2006 and didn't begin working again until May 2007, that would show up as an eight-month gap in your work history. Instead, by including years only, you can show that you left one job in 2006 and began the next in 2007. For all the resume screener knows (unless you are asked in the interview), you ended your previous job on December 31 and began the next one on January 1.

In my more than 15 years of writing thousands of resumes, I've discovered that listing years rather than months and years is a much more effective approach.

Following are a variety of work history challenges faced by job searchers and the strategies that worked well for them.

"I have gaps in my work history."

Milly had worked off and on in her adult life, spending chunks of time as an at-home parent. To present 5 to 15 years of responsible activity, we included this information in her work history and listed her volunteer work at her son's school as "Support Specialist":

WORK HISTORY
- **Support Specialist,** Wilson School District, 2003–Present
- **At-Home Parent,** 2002
- **Service Manager,** Stamp World, 2000–2001
- **At-home Parent,** 1995–2000
- **Office Manager,** Bladell & Company, Inc., 1990–1995

Note: Do you have gaps in your work history that are difficult to account for, such as during a time of illness? If at all possible, do your best to recall anything productive you were doing during that time. For example, if you were volunteering occasionally at your church, you can list this in your work history as follows:

Support Specialist, Name of Church, Year–Year

Or perhaps you were studying a topic on your own, such as learning how to use a computer program. In this case, you could report on how you used your time as the following:

Computer Student, Self-Study, Year–Year

And a widely used fill-in-the-gap strategy is to explain your lack of work as a sabbatical—a planned break you took from work—presented this way:

Sabbatical, Year–Year

However you choose to address the gap in your work history, be sure to account for the time somehow. Otherwise, resume screeners may pass over your resume because they have concerns about your stability as a potential employee.

"I'm making a career change."

For several years, Tristan managed a local restaurant, but now she's pursuing a new career as a personal trainer. Because she's currently completing an online course in personal training, we included this information in her work history, painting a picture of where her career future is headed. We were also able to mention the part-time volunteer training she did as a student in college. This results in an overall impression of Tristan's background as a Personal Trainer, rather than a Restaurant Manager:

> ➤ **Personal Trainer** (Student), National Academy of Sports Medicine, 2006–Present
> ➤ **Manager,** Good Eats, 2004–Present
> ➤ **Student Athletic Trainer,** Lake Forest Athletic Department, 1999–2003
> *Work history also includes numerous part-time summer assignments. Details provided on request.*

"I have more than 20 years of work experience."

Frank worked as a lawyer for nearly 30 years in his own practice. He decided to shift into a career in sales. We didn't want to highlight that he'd begun his work in the 1970s, because it would have made him look too old on paper. Instead, we described his years in law practice as "10+":

- **Sales, Customer Service,** Midline Service Corp., 2007–Present
- **Sales, Legal Advising:** Peak Family Law Practice, 10+ years (ended 2007)

"I've worked for only one employer for a long time."

Cheri had a 20+ year career with one employer, yet she'd held various positions during her time with the company. To add interest and variety to her work history, we detailed her different roles, and instead of listing *all* her assignments, we included a note at the end of the list offering to provide additional work history if requested:

➢ **Business Development Strategist,** IBC, Imaging & Printing Group, 2004–2007
➢ **Program Manager/Customer Support,** IBC, Consumer & Retail, 2002–2004
➢ **Team Manager,** IBC, North American Marketing Center, 1998–2002
➢ **Business Analyst,** IBC, Information Storage Americas, 1996–1998
Additional Work History Provided on Request

"I have just a little experience in my chosen career field."

Kim spent her first years after college working as an international customer relations specialist, yet her true love was in planning and organizing events. After earning a certificate in wedding planning, she decided to pursue her goal of working full time as an event organizer. Because she had been volunteering to plan events for friends and family members since 2005, we were able to describe her as an "Event Coordinator" in her work history:

WORK HISTORY
Event Coordinator, *Part-Time Consulting,* 2005–Present
International Account Manager, *Hill Company,* 2001–Present
Teller, *First Bank,* 2000–2001

"I have had several short-term jobs, and I'm afraid I look like a job hopper."

For a number of reasons (moving, family demands, challenging bosses), Mary had held several short-term positions, many of which were six months or less. Instead of listing them individually and risking her looking too much like a job hopper, we combined similar assignments under a single job title and grouped multiple employers within one time period. We also mentioned her experience as a registered nurse yet didn't provide details about the years worked:

WORK HISTORY & EXPERTISE

➤ **Psychotherapist / Clinical Social Worker**
Naval Hospital Camp Pendleton / Naval Medical Center 2005–2008
➤ **Case Manager / Psychotherapist**
Pleasant Valley Hospital / Mountain Care / Senior Counseling Center, 2003–2004
➤ **Case Manager**
Interfaith Support Services / Jewish Family Center, 1999–2002
➤ **Hospice Social Worker / Case Manager**
Hospice of North Coast / Age Concerns, 1996–1999
➤ **Registered Nurse**—*Details provided on request*

"I have the experience they want but haven't ever held the specific job title."

This was the situation Cory faced. He didn't possess an official engineering degree, yet he had been performing mechanical engineering work in his last position. Instead of listing his exact job title (Engineering Technician), we instead listed the *role* he performed. Note that his work history doesn't say "Mechanical Engineer" (a title) but rather "Mechanical Engineer*ing*" (a function performed). This slight difference can make a huge difference in how resume screeners will perceive Cory's background, viewing him as more of an Engineer rather than a Technician. Listing a function rather than a title provides greater flexibility in presenting specific aspects of your background:

> ➤ **Mechanical Engineering,** *MedInstruments, Inc.*, 1999–2006
> ➤ **Mechanical Engineering Design,** *Hitek Solutions*, 1997–1998
> ➤ **Technician,** *CSU Veterinary Teaching Hospital*, Nuclear Medicine, 1994–1996
> ➤ **Opto-Electronics Technician,** *United States Air Force*, 1990–1994

Organize Your Own Work History

Now it's time to put together your own work history. The following example demonstrates a thought process for pulling together this section.

Let's say, for instance, that you've listed the following as your work history:

- Inventory Specialist, Mighty Manufacturers, Inc., 2006–Present

- Administrative Assistant, Lawn Growers Company, 2001–2003

- Customer Service Representative, Teleservices, Inc., 2000–2001

...and you've listed this information related to your education:

- Associates of Science Degree in Construction Management, Peak Community College, 2006–2008 (completed 2008)

- Student, Richardson High School, 1998–2002

...this info connected to volunteering:

- Sunday School Teacher, First Church, 2004–Present

- Parent Helper, Young Minds Preschool, 2006–Present

...and finally, these details that fall into the "Other" category:

- At-Home Parent, 2003–2007

Let's say that your career target is to land a position as an Assistant Construction Project Manager (you just finished your degree, and now you want to use it!) So, how can you present select pieces of your background while showing 5 to 15 years of responsible activity, not looking like too much of a job hopper, addressing any timeline gaps, and relating your background to your career target? Here's one way to accomplish these goals:

- Materials Specialist, Mighty Manufacturers, Inc., 2006–Present

- Construction Management Student, Peak Community College, 2006–2008

- At-Home Parent, 2003–2007

- Service Coordinator, Lawn Growers Company, 2001–2003

Notice how we've chosen to present certain information: Instead of using the title "Inventory Specialist" with Mighty Manufacturers, we changed it to "Materials Specialist." Why? Because the term "materials" is more closely aligned to the construction industry than is the word "inventory." Yet in the big picture, they basically mean the same thing and can therefore be interchanged.

For the years 2006–2008, we noted that you were a "Construction Management Student." These keywords are directly related to your career target, so it helps to include them prominently in your work history listing. They also help fill a gap in your history for when you were working as an at-home parent.

On this topic, we did include a specific line item detailing what you were doing with your time from 2003–2007. For the most part, resume screeners have no problem with candidates who take a break from their careers to provide at-home care, yet it is important to account for the time frame on your resume so that they don't assume the worst (such as "Was this person in prison?").

Keeping your position target in mind helps you strategically select pieces of your work history and present them in a way that will help you best accomplish your career goals.

Why It's Worth Doing

The Work History section is an essential part of pretty much *every* resume. Just as you expect to see an engine in most any car you would consider buying, resume screeners are looking for the basic component of your work history in your document.

However, just as marketers aim to present product information to us in ways that build interest and motivate us to buy, you'll want to present your work history information in a way that is appealing to resume screeners. Sometimes this means describing the role you played (rather than your exact job title), omitting or highlighting certain pieces of your history, or including school or volunteer experiences as part of this section.

Presenting your work history in line with your career goal and the key skill areas of your chosen specialty helps position you ahead of the competition.

Career Champ Profile: Danielle

After serving as pastor of a small church for more than 10 years, Danielle made the tough decision to switch back into a career in sales so that she could earn more money to save for retirement. On her resume, she wanted to be careful not to show too many years of work history (she's in her mid-50s) and also to highlight her former successes in sales. Because she has co-owned a family window installation business with her sons since 2004 and has provided sales and service support off and on, she was able to list a current sales position. She played down her work as a pastor to provide greater emphasis of her sales expertise. The following resume helped her successfully move into a higher paying position in sales.

Danielle Jones   *Sales / Account Management*
939 Nells Dr.
Loveland, CO 80538
(970) 444-2222, DanielleJones@comcast.net

Accomplished, effective Sales & Business Development Professional with a proven track record for achieving goals and attaining impressive sales results; possess proven skills in effective approaches to target and connect with potential buyers; offer expertise in establishing new customer relationships and growing existing accounts; background includes track record in successful B2B professional sales; deliver a total commitment to quality, service, and customer satisfaction; strengths include superior verbal, written, and presentation skills, with an ability to connect effectively with decision makers; Proficient in Microsoft Office and other computer applications; goal-driven, self-motivated, and disciplined.

WORK EXPERIENCE

- ➢ **Business Development,** Windows-In!, 2004–Present
  Concurrently pastor of Calvary Apostolic Church, 1994–2007
- ➢ **Sales / Account Management,** Solid Wood Products, 1992–1994
- ➢ **Sales / Account Management,** SafeHome Insurance, 1990–1992

Sales & Account Management Expertise...

- • Implemented innovative, effective prospecting techniques targeting profitable niche markets, with excellent results:
  - ✓ **Achieved Top Producer sales status.**
- • Attained steady business growth through consistent prospecting, account development, and delivery of exceptional customer service.
- • **Increased business sales by 44% in one year** through strategic analysis of market opportunities and implementation of effective business development techniques.
- • Expanded sales from local to countrywide scale by establishing sales relationships with national retail chain stores:
  - ✓ **Grew sales volume by 1,000% within two years.**

Client Relationship & Teamwork Skills...

- • Possess outstanding ability to connect with prospects and customers, determine needs and priorities, and develop long-term win-win relationships.
- • Currently completing advanced studies in Organizational Development, gaining **valuable skills in sales and motivation.**
- • Offer strengths in presentations and consulting to support the sales process, and resulting in a high rate of referral business.

EDUCATION

- • Masters of Arts, Organizational Leadership , Regent University, *In Progress*
- • Bachelor of Arts, Theology, Christian Life College

Figure 7.1: Danielle's resume.

Core Courage Concept

Presenting your work history differently can feel risky. Will you do it "right"? What will potential employers say? Yet by staying focused on your career goal and strategically selecting and presenting pieces of your work history, you can greatly increase the results your resume generates. Trying things differently is worthwhile, even if it makes you a little nervous. That nervousness will be replaced by excitement and pride when your resume helps you achieve your career goal.

Confidence Checklist

- ☐ Create lists of your work history components.
- ☐ Consider options for how to present your information.
- ☐ Organize your own work history.

Chapter 8

Develop a Dynamite Education Section

How does your education support your career goals? Education, like Work History, can be presented in a variety of ways. In this chapter, you learn how to portray the most important aspects of your training to their maximum advantage, moving your resume one step further ahead — and you one step closer to achieving your career goals.

Risk It or Run From It?

- **Risk Rating:** About the same risk level as creating your Work History section: Important but not too difficult to execute.

- **Payoff Potential:** Because Education is also considered as a "must have" section in your resume, including this information—and presenting it as effectively as possible—can help launch your resume to the top of the "Interview this person!" pile.

- **Time to Complete:** 15 to 20 minutes.

- **Bailout Strategy:** Come back to this section later, have someone else create it for you, or find an Education section example you like and copy it, filling in your own information.

(continued)

(continued)

> - **The "20 Percent Extra" Edge:** An effective Education section adds credibility to your background. Being thoughtful about how to best present your training can give you a valuable edge over your competition.
>
> - **"Go for It!" Bonus Activity:** Survey a few decision makers about what they perceive to be essential educational components related to your career target. Then evaluate your own Education section to determine ways to address any gaps or opportunities.

How to Create an Effective Education Section

It's highly likely that you've lived through a number of educational experiences, from the classes you completed in high school, to surviving the school of hard knocks. These pieces of your past can be strategically presented to help you create an awesome resume that moves you toward your career goals.

List Details About Your Education and Training

When you're building your Education section, your goal should be to present a level of training, certifications, and/or degrees that are a good match for the career target you're pursuing, without coming across as over- or undereducated.

To accomplish this, begin by making some notes about your education and training history. This is just a rough-draft listing of what you've acquired, so don't worry about making it "perfect" right now. Fill in the following tables, keeping in mind that your listings may include any of the following:

- Completed degrees and certifications

- Attendance at a community college, university, or training school (even if you didn't complete your studies)

- Professional development seminars

- Self-study experiences

To help with your decision making, also refer to the experiences inventory you created in chapter 3, as well as the objective you chose in chapter 4, and the key skill areas and relevant experience you defined in chapters 5 and 6.

Begin by listing any formal education or certification training you've received:

Most Recent Formal Training	Name of Institution	Degree/Program name
Next Most Recent	Name of Institution	Degree/Program name
Next Most Recent	Name of Institution	Degree/Program name

Next, note any specific classes or workshops you've attended, particularly those that are related to your position target:

Workshop/Class Attended	Name of Institution
Workshop/Class Attended	Name of Institution
Workshop/Class Attended	Name of Institution

Now list any informal training you've had, such as a time when you received instruction from someone demonstrating a specific technique, or when you taught yourself something, particularly if it's related to your career target:

Informal Training
Informal Training
Informal Training

Now you're going to consider which pieces of your education to include and how to present them to your best advantage.

Choose the Education Section Format That Best Supports Your Career Goals

Following are examples of Education sections created by several job searchers, as well as the challenges they faced. Review these examples to decide which techniques are best suited to your individual situation.

You'll notice that in some cases, the year of completion (or anticipated completion) is listed. In other cases, it's not. My suggested guidelines for deciding whether to include the dates are these:

- If you've recently completed a training program or degree, it's often a good idea to include the date.

- If you've been a student for the past few years and were not employed, it's a good idea to list dates of education, to account for what you've been doing with your time.

- If the date of your graduation is more than five years ago, don't include it.

"I have some college, but I never completed my degree."
Remember Cory from chapter 7? He's the job hunter with the mechanical engineering experience but no formal degree to back it up. Although he doesn't have a formal degree in engineering, he has completed a number of technical training courses related to his specialty. This was how he presented his Education section.

Education, Associations & Professional Development

- Bachelors Studies, Colorado State University

- SPIE (International Society for Optical Engineering) Coursework:
  - SC013—Principles for Mounting Optical Components (Yoder, Jr.)
  - SC014—Introduction to Optomechanical Design
  - SC015—Structural Adhesives for Optical Bonding
  - SC219—Materials: Properties and Fabrication for Stable Optics

- Additional Engineering Coursework:
  - MCAD of Denver courses in SolidWorks Sheetmetal, SolidWorks Advanced Assembly Modeling, COSMOS FloWorks, COSMOSWorks Professional (member of COSUG)
  - Advanced Excel Training
  - Geometric Dimensioning and Tolerancing (GD&T)—ANSI Y14.5M
  - Electronics Technical Training, United States Air Force

"I have *lots* of education—maybe too much!"

Dora was making a career shift from a career in nursing to pursue work as a Human Resources Specialist. She possesses master's, bachelor's, and associate's degrees in nursing and is currently completing a second master's degree in business. She decided to play down her nursing degrees, to put more emphasis on her HR-related training.

EDUCATION & TRAINING:

- **MBA, University of Phoenix** (anticipated graduation 2009)
  Relevant coursework:
  - <u>Organizational Development</u>: Employee motivation, group dynamics, change theory, organizational culture, diversity
  - <u>Legal Environment of Business</u>: Employment law, legal due diligence, analytical problem solving
- **Equal Employment Opportunity Counselor Training & Mediation Certification**
- **Masters, Bachelors, and Associates Degrees in Nursing** (*details on request*)

"I don't have any formal education."

Lisa was creating her resume to support her job search for an office support position. Since she completed high school, her only additional training was two one-day training courses at a community college. We presented her education this way, adopting the "less is more" approach.

EDUCATION

- **Western State College,** Communications & Business Coursework

"I'm changing careers. What parts of my education make sense for me to include?"

Colin worked for more than 20 years as a Finance Specialist in high tech and was now switching into a career as an Organizational Consultant. Because consultants frequently have graduate degrees, it made sense for Colin to provide details about both his degrees.

EDUCATION

- **M.S. Accounting,** Colorado State University
- **B.S. Microbiology,** Colorado State University

Colin was also interested in creating a resume that would allow him to find a low-key, in-between job as he searched for a higher level consulting position, so he also created a "barebones" resume (see the examples in the appendix) that played down his graduate-level education.

EDUCATION

- **B.S. Microbiology,** Colorado State University
  Additional graduate work in accounting studies. Details provided on request.

"I just graduated from my training program."

Riley recently completed his training as a Motorcycle Technician. We listed his education this way and positioned it near the top of his resume.

EDUCATION & INTERESTS

- **Motorcycle Technician Specialist** ("Professional" Designation), 3.83 GPA *Motorcycle Mechanics Institute,* Phoenix, AZ.
- **Graduate,** *Windsor High School*
- **Hobbies:** *Motocross, snowmobiling, snowboarding, camping, and boating*

As you can see, there are many ways to put together an Education section, depending on your career objective. Now it's time to compose yours!

Panic Point! Career Cowards sometimes wonder, "Don't I need to list *all* my education to be honest about my training, even if it's not related to my career target?" Does it bother you not to include every single course and degree you've completed? Although you may feel as though you need to list *everything,* keep in mind that most resumes are quickly scanned (you typically get about 7 to 10 seconds of the reader's attention!), and including *too* much educational information—especially if it's not related to your career target—can be distracting. One strategy is to title this section "Related Education" and include only your relevant educational details.

Select and Present Key Components of Your Education

How will you put together your Education section? Walk through the following hypothetical situation to help in your composing process.

Let's say that you've listed the following as pieces of your educational history:

Formal Training:

B.S. Communications, University of Tennessee

A few graduate courses toward a master's in Public Relations

Workshops/Classes Attended:

"Conflict Resolution," a one-day training course offered through work

"MS Word Advanced Skills," a two-day training class at the local community college

"Writing Love Poems," a six-week course offered through your city recreation program

"Poetry Development," a semester long, online certificate course in teaching poetry writing through Open Mind University

Self-Study/Informal Training:

Someone at work taught you how to develop simple web pages.

You've spent quite a bit of time writing poetry on your own.

Your aim is to create a resume that will highlight your background for teaching a community college course in writing poetry. Here's one way to present training information in the Education section.

EDUCATION & TRAINING

❖ **Poetry Development**, <u>Teaching Certificate</u>, Open Mind University.
  o   Selected coursework:
    ▪ *Helping Students Choose and Develop Poetry Topics*
    ▪ *Overcoming Writer's Block*
    ▪ *Coaching Students on Poetry Writing Improvement*
❖ **"Writing Love Poems,"** Pleasantville Continuing Education Program
❖ **M.S. Public Relations,** Regal University, *partial completion*
❖ **B.S. Communications,** University of Tennessee

In this example, the poetry-related experience is listed first. We also mentioned partial work toward a master's degree because an advanced degree is often preferred for teaching positions. We didn't include training in conflict resolution and Excel, because while valuable, they're not specifically related to your position target.

Now it's your turn to put together a draft of your Education section. While you may feel nervous about choosing and listing specific information, keep in mind that you can always come back and modify the information later…but for now, at least get it started!

Why It's Worth Doing

Like Work History, Education is considered by most resume screeners to be an essential section in a resume. Skip it, and you may raise unnecessary concerns about your background. "Does this person have any education at all? Would we be taking too much of a risk to interview him?" Although you may not have the ideal education, chances are very good that you have *some* training that supports your target career.

By aiming to match your training to the level desired for the position, you improve your chances for being considered as a qualified candidate, moving you closer to achieving your career goals.

Career Champ Profile: Peter

Peter (presented as P.R. in his confidential resume) was seeking a position as a chemist. Within his specialty, extensive certifications and training are a big career plus, so it made sense to provide lots of details in his resume's Education section.

Core Courage Concept

You're moving step by step toward developing an effective resume. By building your Education section, you've completed another key component. Are you sweating a little? You may be…this is hard work! But keep pushing forward, and before you know it, you'll have created an outstanding career tool for yourself.

P.R.
Wyoming
E-mail: prwy@msn.com
Phone: (307) 444-2222

Science Officer /
Analytical Chemist

Experienced, qualified Science Officer and Analytical Chemist with laboratory experience in Chemical, Biological, Radiological, Nuclear, and High Yield Explosive (CBRNE) identification, process stream analysis, quality assurance, bench chemistry, and Federal/State hazardous material regulatory compliance; able to plan and conduct development of analytical methodology for detection, identification, and characterization of chemical agents, including degradation, decontamination, and demilitarization products, intermediates, precursors, simulants, other hazardous material and pollutants; possess excellent track record in project management.

WORK EXPERIENCE

Nuclear Medical Science Officer (NMSO), *Weapons of Mass Destruction Civil Support Team* (WMD-CST), DEPARTMENT OF DEFENSE, UNITED STATES ARMY, 2000–Present

- Work in National and State Biological and Chemical Warfare Laboratories and operate mobile Analytical Laboratory System (ALS).
- Maintain rigorous support of proper methodologies and related protocols for sample processing:
  - Glove box, GC/MS, FTIR, PCR, Gamma Spectra Interpretation, and Microscopy (Gram Stain, Fluorescence, and Polarized Light)
- Write analytical standard operating procedures and verify equipment capabilities with live BW/CW agents and TIC/TIMs, and train emergency responders on CBRNE remediation techniques.
- Select Accomplishments:
  - Successfully led three teams through Secretary of Defense certification.
  - Responded to 25 missions involving CBRNE.
  - Trained unit and adjacent agencies in hazard mitigation and laboratory analyses.

Senior Project Chemist/Interim Supervisor, XT INDUSTRIES, INC., 1992–1999
Plant analyses and maintenance of laboratory equipment supporting nitrogen fertilizer production

- Supervised laboratory technicians and chemists.
- Analyzed product and process stream compositions:
  - Ammonia, Urea, Urea Ammonia Nitrate (UAN), and Nitric Acid
- Maintained, repaired, and automated laboratory equipment:
  - GC, IC, AA, FTIR, GC/MS, UV/VIS, pH, Turbidity, Densitometer, Refractometer, Conductivity Meters, Coulometric, Potentiometric, and Volumetric Titrators
- Handled data acquisition, accumulation, and reporting; monitored effluent discharge, prepared State Discharge Monitoring Reports (DMR), manifested wastes.
- Select Accomplishments:
  - Completed 10 EPA Air Emission Stack Tests.
  - Supervised sample testing of 10 chemical plants with excellent results.
  - Worked on 4 Total Quality Management (TQM) teams.
  - Helped install the Laboratory Information Management System.

EDUCATION

- **MS—Science for Domestic Response,** Indiana University in Pennsylvania, GPA: 3.5
- **BS—Chemistry,** University of Louisiana in Monroe
  Detailed listing of training and certifications on following page

Figure 8.1: Peter's resume.

P.R.
Resume page 2 of 2
E-mail: prwy@msn.com
Phone: (307) 444-2222

TRAINING & CERTIFICATIONS

Laboratory Equipment Certifications:

- GC/MS (liquid, headspace, and SPME injections)—Inficon Hapsite, Agilent
- Troubleshooting and Maintenance for the HP5890/HP6890 GC Systems
- Ion Chromatograph—Dionex
- Real Time and Traditional Gel Electrophoresis PCR—Idaho Tech
- FTIR (ATR and ARO)—Smith Detection HazmatID, TravelIR, and IluminatIR
- McCrone Research Institute—Advance Polarized Light Microscopy, White Powder Identification, Fourier Transform Infra-Red and Fluorescence Microscopy

Hazardous Material Certifications and Specialized CBRNE Training:

- WMD Agent Identification and Production Training (Chemical, Biological, and Radiological): Lawrence Livermore National Laboratory, Dugway Proving Ground, Nuclear Defense Weapons School, and WMD Response Element Advanced Laboratory Integrated Training and Indoctrination (REALITI) Program graduate
- EPA: Emergency Response to HAZMAT Incident, HAZMAT Technician Level (165.15), Safety and Health Decision Making for Managers (165.8)
- FBI/CIA/Local Law Enforcement: FBI Crime Scene Awareness, Federal Integration and Evidence Preservation at a WMD Incident Site, CIA Small Scale Production, Emergency Vehicle Operation
- DoD/DOJ/CDC/VA: CWA and BWA production, Biological Warfare and Terrorism: The Military and Public Response, Domestic Preparedness Senior Official's and WMD Incident Measured Response, Field and Medical Management of Chemical and Biological Casualties, Medical Nuclear Biological Chemical (NBC) Readiness Workshop, Psychological Effects from a WMD Incident: From Incident to Management, Hospital Emergency ICS, VA WMD, Dugway Proving Ground Raid Thrust, Emergency Response to Domestic Biological Incidents, EMS Concepts for WMD, Terrorism Awareness for Emergency First Responders, ServSafe Certification, Defense Nuclear Weapons School Radiological Accident Command, Control and Coordination
- Army Medical Department (AMEDD) Education: Army Preventive Medicine and Environmental Science, Industrial Hygiene, Medical Management of Chemical and Biological Casualties, Medical Effects of Ionization Radiation, Transport of Biomedical Material, National Registry EMT-B

Computer / Information Systems:

- Served on the CFI computer network and programming team.
- Installed Vulcan Laboratory Information Management System (LIMS).
- Proficient in Windows, MS Office (Access, Excel, Word, and PowerPoint).

ASSOCIATIONS & AWARDS

- American Chemical Society
- Numerous Army and Air Force Achievement and Commendation Medals
- John S. Ring Exceptional Leadership and Service Award

Confidence Checklist

- ☐ List details about your education and training.
- ☐ Choose the Education section format that best supports your career goals.
- ☐ Select and present key components of your education.

Chapter 9

Give Your Resume
an "Extra" Boost

I f you want to give your resume an edge over your competition, consider adding in a few "extras" to help set it apart. A few well-chosen achievements, affiliations, awards, and hobbies may be just what it takes to raise your resume to the top of the "Interview This Person!" pile.

Risk It or Run From It?

- **Risk Rating:** Very low risk. This chapter could even be classified as "fun"!

- **Payoff Potential:** Excellent. Brainstorming and including some well-chosen "extras" can elevate your resume from "good" to "great!"

- **Time to Complete:** 30 minutes or so.

- **Bailout Strategy:** Technically, you don't need to include "extras," and you can flip right by the chapter. However, you may cheat yourself of some fantastic strategies for raising your resume to the next level of excellence. At least take a few minutes to skim the information presented here.

(continued)

(continued)

- **The "20 Percent Extra" Edge:** You know when you see someone at an event who looks especially great and stands out from the crowd? Perhaps he chose just the right tie, or she wore the perfect shoes. Yet that simple addition made a huge difference in his or her appearance! That's what the following extras can do for your resume.

- **"Go for It!" Bonus Activity:** If you worry that you're lacking in the necessary qualifications for your career target, then consider joining a relevant professional association right now and becoming active in a few of its activities. This new membership will provide you with some instant qualification-building "extras" that you can include on your resume!

How to Decide Which (and If) Extras Are Right for You

Awards…accomplishments…hobbies…associations…does it make sense for you to include these pieces of information in your resume? It might! Read through the following descriptions of resume "extras," along with examples of each, and then decide if they have a place in your resume.

Consider a Range of "Extra" Options

Years ago, job searchers would regularly list their height, weight, and even the names of their children in their resumes. Today, however, including that kind of personal information is pretty rare (unless, of course, you are a model promoting your physical attributes!).

While your weight most likely doesn't have a place in your resume, new "extra" pieces of information are now popping up. Any of the following pieces of data could be included in yours:

- **Accomplishments/Achievements:** Did you consistently meet all your performance goals in your last position? Or maybe you helped the company grow its profitability by 20 percent?

Perhaps you showed up on time for work for two straight years. Or you earned the reputation as the "walking encyclopedia" with one employer because you could quickly recall a multitude of product and customer details. All these items could be considered as accomplishments, and chances are very good that you've achieved a number of valuable successes that may have a place in your resume.

- **Affiliations/Associations:** Are you a member of a community recycling group? A ski club? A professional organization of accountants? How about a local church, college sorority, or worker's union? Your affiliations may be a beneficial resume addition.

- **Hobbies:** Love to knit, hunt, take pictures, or run? Does the resume screener want to know about your interests? In some cases, yes!

- **Awards:** Were you once named "Employee of the Month" or crowned "Manager of the Year"? Listing these honors in your resume may serve you well.

- **Photo:** Would sharing your photo with an employer buy you a competitive edge? Under the right circumstances, absolutely! If appearance is especially important in your profession—such as in sales, broadcasting, or as a spokesperson of a particular product or service—including a photo may make sense for you.

- **Personal Stats:** Are you fantastically fit? Does the resume reader care? Perhaps...especially if strength and stamina are essential to the job.

View and Consider "Extra" Examples

So what "extras" might you include in your resume? Take a peek at the following add-ons as possible inclusions in your own documents.

Achievements

Achievements can be gleaned from a variety of sources—from precise data noted in your annual performance review to a casual comment from a customer about your outstanding service. Bruce listed the following accomplishments in his resume:

- Currently oversee operation of $3.5M hotel facility that achieved top performance ranking from among 500+ facilities for growth, profitability, and customer satisfaction.

- Led property to top-performer status in market for six consecutive years through a dedicated focus on Continuous Quality Improvement.

- Achieved annual revenue growth averaging 8% per year in a highly competitive industry while attaining 42% profitability margins.

- Possess demonstrated expertise in launching new facilities: Opened hotels that earned top corporate ranking within the first year.

And Joann listed these in hers:

- Completed comprehensive cold-calling training seminar and successfully completed more than 1,400 phone calls to set sales appointments.

- In a 12-month period, reviewed 15,000 work orders while maintaining a very high (99.5%) accuracy record.

- Consistently achieved high marks on performance reviews for ability to perform effectively in teams.

Affiliations/Associations

Your connection to a particular group or association can build your credibility in the eyes of a decision maker and also position you as a team player and community-minded contributor. Ann listed these affiliations on her resume:

- Member, American Counseling Association, Society for Human Resources Development, and Northern Colorado Human Resources Association

- Member, Colorado Renewable Energy Society and Partners for Youth

Hobbies

Could your love of music give you an edge over other job searchers? Possibly, especially if the resume screener is a fan, also. Pete mentioned his participation in a band on his resume...and a hiring manager interviewed him because, as he said, "Anyone who can get along with band members for that long would probably do well in our chaotic work environment":

- Lead guitarist, "The Purple Bear," since 2000

Awards

Have you been recognized by others for your excellence? Noting this information in your resume offers an effective way to help you stand out among your competition. Sam, a sales manager, included these awards in his resume.

Management & Leadership Excellence:
  ✓ Awarded "**Manager of the Year**" from among more than 90 managers company wide.
  ✓ Received **"President's Award for Outstanding Service"** for participation in youth mentoring program.
  ✓ Earned Four **Dale Carnegie Excellence Awards** for performance.

Photos and Images

Would an image—either a photo of you, a visual of an item you designed or built, or a picture representing something important to you—boost your resume's effectiveness? Depending on the situation, it could! Riley, the just-graduated job searcher mentioned in chapter 8, included this clip-art photo he found on the Internet to emphasize his interest in motorcycles:

Personal Stats

Are you "Five foot two...eyes of blue..." and does it make sense to say so in your resume? If physical attributes are a make-it-or-break-it factor in your line of work, feel free to list important personal information if it will help you to appear better qualified. Ben, a personal assistant and bodyguard, included this information in his resume:

- 6'4", 200 lbs., extremely fit

Decide on "Extras" That Are Right for You

The following guidelines and development suggestions will help you decide which, if any, extras to include. Referring to the experiences inventory you created in chapter 3, as well as the objective you chose in chapter 4, and key skill areas and relevant experience you listed in chapters 5 and 6 will also be a big help.

Accomplishments/Achievements

I've never met a resume that couldn't benefit from the addition of an achievement or two, so you can feel safe developing and including a few of your own. Although building in a few accomplishments is pretty much always a good idea, I know from experience that resume writers often struggle with identifying a few they want to include.

Panic Point! Career Cowards frequently worry, "Do I even have any accomplishments worth mentioning?" Unless you've chosen to do *absolutely nothing* with your life for a long, long time (and I doubt you would be reading this book if you were that type of person), you've accomplished things. Before you throw this book under the dirty clothes in your closet, panicked at the thought of identifying some accomplishments, take a deep breath. Then tell yourself, "Including accomplishments in my resume is an 'extra'...I don't need to get myself all worked up over this. But just for fun, I'm going to do my best to identify a few potential accomplishments, and then I'll decide if they're worth mentioning."

Following is a technique for brainstorming potential accomplishments to include:

1. Review the key skill areas for your target position (the ones you developed in chapter 5), as well as the experiences inventory you created in chapter 3.

2. Ask yourself, "In which of these key skill areas have I demonstrated some significant success?" It will probably help for you to review your experiences inventory to remind yourself of important events and activities in your life.

3. Keep an open mind about what can be classified as an achievement. You don't need to have accomplished some world-changing feat for an achievement to count. As long as you performed an activity in a quality way, there's a good chance it

can be presented as an accomplishment. For instance, effectively serving several customers each day over a period of months can be presented like this:

- Successfully responded to the needs of approximately 50 customers per day, over a period of six months, resulting in satisfied clients, repeat business, and compliments for service provided.

4. When you hit upon potential accomplishments, develop them into achievements you can include in your resume by asking yourself, "What evidence do I have that I executed this task well? Did I help save money? Make money? Improve quality? Improve the organization's image? What were the results?

Challenge yourself to develop at least five accomplishments that you might include in your resume.

> **Note:** Want to put even more time and effort into brainstorming accomplishments? Then check out chapters 4 and 5 in *The Career Coward's Guide to Interviewing,* an awesome companion book to this one. In those chapters, I go into even greater detail on how to brainstorm and develop your accomplishments into content that can be used in resumes and interviews.

Affiliations/Associations

Which groups are you a part of, formally or informally, either currently or in the past? They may include

- Professional or industry associations
- Community service or nonprofit organizations
- Hobby or special interest clubs
- Church or religious groups

Brainstorm a list before you decide which ones it makes sense to include. For example, my brainstormed list of organizations and affiliations includes these: National Career Development Association, American Counseling Association, National Resume Writers Association, Career Masters Institute, First United Methodist Church, National Charity League, Poudre School District Volunteers, University of Tennessee Alumni, Colorado State University Alumni, Old Town Yoga, and an informal group of inline skaters.

As a next step, ask yourself, "Would my resume be strengthened by mentioning any of these? On the flip side, would my resume be harmed or weakened by including any of them?" Some of the answers to these questions will be obvious. Including the career counseling and resume-writing associations, for instance, would increase my credibility if I were aiming for a position as a career counselor/resume writer. But does it make sense to list my church? If the resume screener dislikes Methodists (and some people do!), then I'd be booted into the "No, Thank You!" pile quickly. *However,* if it's important to me to work with people who accept my faith, then I wouldn't mind being screened out by someone who doesn't.

Would I want to include information about my volunteer work, my college alumni associations, or my inline skating group? Those are fairly inoffensive, so I could choose to go either way with them. Maybe I'd include them if I had extra space.

As you can see, it's not a clearcut process deciding which affiliations to include, but here are some guidelines to consider:

> *Include affiliation information if a) it clearly supports your career target, and b) you don't mind being judged for your connection to that group.*

Check out the Career Champ resume in this chapter for a good example of these recommendations. Richard is an active member of the National Rifle Association, an organization that elicits strong negative reactions from many people. Yet Richard chose to list this information on his resume because he's aiming for a management position with a store that sells outdoorsman gear. Including the NRA makes sense in this case!

Hobbies and Special Interest Clubs

The same principles you would use to help you decide which affiliations to include also apply to choices you might make regarding your hobbies and special interests.

It's your choice if you want to include dates of membership. My personal preference is to leave off dates because they clutter the resume and typically aren't that important to the decision maker.

Awards

You can most likely recall any awards you've received. List them and, once again, decide how relevant they are to your career target. An award like "Employee of the Month" is fairly generic and would most likely strengthen any resume. On the flip side, it probably wouldn't make sense for me to include the graphic design award I won in college because I'm not pursuing graphic design work!

And similar to the associations, affiliations, and special interest groups, include dates if you want or just leave them off.

Photos and Images

Will your resume benefit from including a photo or image? Most resumes don't need images and may in fact be ruined by the addition of one. Although you want your resume to stand out among the competition, you don't want it to look *too* different, and including a picture or graphic can push it over the edge into "too weird" territory! The small percentage of resumes that will benefit from including an image usually fall into these categories:

- Job searchers who are seeking an artsy or creative job, such as with an advertising agency.

- Individuals who are aiming for a position that is very image conscious, such as modeling or even pharmaceutical sales.

- People who are fanatically avid about their specialty and can demonstrate this through a related picture (see Richard's Career Champ resume in this chapter).

Otherwise, it's safer to skip the photo.

Personal Stats

The same reasoning for including photos and images applies to the inclusion of personal stats, so use your best judgment.

After you've created your list of potential "extras" to include in your resume, compile them in a list to use when you format and build your actual resume.

Panic Point! Worry that including these "extras" in your resume will come across as unprofessional or conceited? Many Career Cowards share your concern. However, it's been my experience that as long as you include extras that are based on *fact* (such as "I really was given the 'Best Problem Solver' award") rather than *opinion* ("I believe I'm the best problem solver in the company"), resume screeners view candidates who include these extras as being stronger candidates.

Why It's Worth Doing

The vast majority of job searchers don't include extras like accomplishments, affiliations, hobbies, and awards in their resumes. Yet by simply including some carefully selected add-ons, you can quickly reroute your resume from the "No, Thank You" to the "Interview This Person!" pile. Want better resume results? Then take the risk and go the "extra" step!

Career Champ Profile: Richard

Richard had developed a successful career as a store manager in the building supplies industry, yet his heart wasn't into plumbing fixtures and cans of paint. Rather, he *loves* hunting and fishing and was aiming to land a store manager position with an organization like Cabella's or Dick's Sporting Goods. A few well-placed extras in his resume communicated this goal clearly and quickly landed Richard interviews—and an offer—with a hunting and fishing store.

RICHARD SPRINGER

600 Apache Way
Fort Collins, CO 80524
(970) 221-5555 email24@hotmail.com

Retail Operations Manager

Accomplished **Retail Operations Manager** with 10+ years experience in maintaining smooth and profitable store operations. Expertise in opening of retail locations and supervision of sales and operations teams and activities; proven strengths in recruiting, hiring, training, and staffing; competent in preparing and interpreting sales and operations reports; skilled in facilities and grounds maintenance; devoted to delivering outstanding customer service; **avid big-game hunter, fisherman, and outdoor enthusiast.**

WORK HISTORY

Retail Operations Manager, THE HOME CENTER, INC., 2001–Present..........................

- Launched opening of store and maintain daily operations of the business, ensuring compliance with corporate, state, and governmental regulations. Monitor and improve processes to maximize store efficiency and profitability. Build productive teams through effective hiring, training, and management systems. Prepare and present financial and business reports. Manage day-to-day flow of product through receiving, stocking, sales, and ordering channels. Serve as merchandising manager for Garden and Paint departments.

Operations Management Accomplishments:

- ➤ **Beat sales goals by 10% in 2004 and 2005,** on annual sales of $29 million.
- ➤ **Kept staff turnover to 1.5%,** for a team of 130 associates.
- ➤ **Maintained 99.5% in-stock conditions** on 30,000 SKUs.
- ➤ **Award-winning for best operational audit scores/results for 2003 + 2004.**

Internal Audit / Inventory Specialist, THE HOME CENTER, INC., 1996–2001....................

- Traveled nationwide and applied performance improvement strategies to enhance project management, strategic risk assessments, process analysis, problem solving, data analysis, operational excellence, and organization development results. Oversee and improve physical inventory processes and results for the company. Worked side-by-side with store, district, and divisional management to monitor counts and cutoffs status and improve inventory processes.

Continued...

Figure 9.1: Richard's resume.

RICHARD SPRINGER

Resume, page 2 of 2
(970) 221-5555 sammarr24@hotmail.com

WORK HISTORY (continued)

District Trainer, THE HOME CENTER, INC., 1995..

- Worked on location at several sites in New Jersey and Pennsylvania, training associates on basic computer skills and operating system fundamentals. Developed materials and curriculum to support training objectives, and collaborated with store and district management to successfully integrate training into day-to-day operations.

  Training Accomplishments:
  - ➤ Successfully trained approximately 800 employees on essential computer skills to support business operations.
  - ➤ Achieved an average of 99% student proficiency, based on performance testing.

Additional work experience with WalBig and Uno Hardware stores. Details provided on request.

EDUCATION

- **Operations and Programming Certificate,** Chubb Institute of Technical Training

SPORTS & GAMING ACCOMPLISHMENTS & AFFILIATIONS

- ➤ 15+ year member, National Rifle Association.
- ➤ Avid outdoorsman for 20+ years.
- ➤ Proficient big-game bow hunter, with numerous elk, deer, turkey, and black bear trophies.
- ➤ Skilled marksman with rifle, shotgun, muzzleloader, and handguns.
- ➤ Possess expertise in fishing, mountaineering, camping, backpacking, skiing, and snowshoeing.
- ➤ Climbed Mt Rainier, highest (14,411′) and most strenuous in the lower 48.
- ➤ Backpacked hundreds of miles of the Appalachian, Centennial, and Continental Divide trails.
- ➤ Award-winning and dominating player in baseball, softball, football, and basketball.
- ➤ Avid outdoor, nature, and wildlife photographer.
- ➤ Willing and able to share interesting stories of outdoor adventures.

Core Courage Concept

Thinking about stepping outside your comfort zone and including some unique extras in your resume? Congratulations! Even though doing so may make you a little nervous, the payoff in increased results is well worth the squirm factor. Write down some possible extras, knowing that ultimately, you'll be the one to decide whether they are included. It can't hurt to brainstorm some ideas. Go for it!

Confidence Checklist

☐ Discover a range of "extra" options.

☐ View and consider "extra" examples.

☐ Decide on "extras" that are right for you.

Chapter 10

Choose the Right Resume Format for You

Chronological, functional, hybrid, or CV…which resume format is right for you? The clear-cut guidelines presented in this chapter will help you make a choice that pulls together the most important elements of your unique skill set and allows you to present that information to achieve your maximum career results.

Risk It or Run From It?

- **Risk Rating:** There's a minor risk in choosing a resume format. Yet keep in mind that you can try out different formats and see which one feels best to you. Later, if you're not pleased with the results you're getting, try another one.

- **Payoff Potential:** Selecting an effective organization plan for your resume can make your entire document come together like a beautiful melody.

- **Time to Complete:** However long it takes you to read this chapter, plus a few minutes to make your choice.

- **Bailout Strategy:** Flip through the examples in this book (and other resume books, if you want more examples), find a format you like, and then copy it.

(continued)

(continued)

- **The "20 Percent Extra" Edge:** Most people put about as much time into thinking how they're going to organize their resume as they do in deciding what they're going to order at the coffee shop. By taking a few extra minutes to weigh the pros and cons of formatting strategies—especially as they relate to your personal career situation—you improve your chances for achieving outstanding results.

- **"Go for It!" Bonus Activity:** Create your resume in more than one format, capitalizing on the benefits of each, and then decide which approach works better for you.

How to Choose a Resume Style That Best Supports Your Career Goals

Just as people dress themselves in outfits as unique as their personality (and no two ensembles are exactly alike), there are infinite ways to organize the information in your resume. As you read through the different approaches in this chapter, keep reminding yourself that there's no single *right* way to organize a resume. Your aim should be to choose an approach that supports your career goals and reflects your distinctive style. The following process will help you decide which organizational approach will help you achieve these objectives.

Learn a Little About Different Resume Formats

In the world of resumes, most documents fall into one of these four organizational formats:

- **Chronological:** As the name implies, this resume format presents information based on a chronology—or timeline—of events. Job searchers who choose a chronological format typically describe their latest position at the top of the list and then work backward in time to explain earlier positions. Examples of chronological resumes are shown on pages 41, 98, and 132 in this book.

- **Functional or Skill-Based:** These terms are used interchange-ably in the resume world. Instead of organizing information chronologically, this style puts the emphasis on functions or skills—typically key skill areas (remember those from chapter 6?). See pages 30, 59, and 70 for examples of resumes organized in a functional or skill-based style.

- **Combined or Hybrid:** Just as the hybrid class of automobiles blends two energy sources, the hybrid resume blends both the chronological and functional/skill-based styles. While not as common a choice as the first two formats described, the hybrid format may be just right for you if none of the other styles seem to fit. An example is shown on page 120.

- **Curriculum Vitae (CV):** A CV is a presentation of profession-al data most often used by teachers, academicians, and other scholarly types. An example of a CV is shown on page 152. Situations in which you need to organize your information in a CV format are pretty clear cut; the employer (typically a col-lege, university, or school system) will specifically request it.

Take a Quick Quiz to See Which Format Will Work Best

To help you decide which resume format will work best for your unique career situation, answer "Yes" or "No" to the following questions:

1. I am planning to stay in the same line of work—either target-ing the same kind of position I held most recently or moving up to the next step within my chosen career.

    __Yes   __No

2. I have stayed in or progressed within my same career path, taking on increasing levels of responsibility from position to position.

    __Yes   __No

3. I am entering a brand-new career field, either as a career changer or a recent graduate just beginning in my profession.

        __Yes   _ No

4. I haven't been in the workforce in the last number of years—either because I was a student, or because I took off time from work to raise children, handle an illness, care for a family member, or for some other reason.

        __Yes   __No

5. I work (or did work) for the same company for more than 10 years and have held multiple positions within that company. The next step I'm targeting in my career will be toward one of those types of positions.

        __Yes   __No

6. My career situation is truly unique and doesn't fall within any of the statements described in the preceding questions.

        __Yes   __No

7. I am aiming for a position as a teacher, professor, or administrator in academia.

        __Yes   __No

Interpret Your Results and Make Your Decision

If you answered Yes to questions 1 or 2, then organizing your resume chronologically is probably the best choice for you.

If you answered Yes to questions 3 or 4, then a functional/skill-based resume is most likely the way to go for you.

If you answered Yes to questions 5 or 6, then consider a hybrid resume format.

If your answer to question 7 was Yes, then opt for a CV format.

Details about these specific formats and how-tos for building your own resume are provided in the next few chapters.

Why It's Worth Doing

Without even thinking, most people automatically organize their resumes in a chronological format. This isn't necessarily a bad thing to do; the vast majority of resumes are prepared in a chronological format, and it's by far the most common type.

Although "common" is okay, a format specifically selected to address your individual career needs—whether it's chronological, functional, hybrid, or CV—will help you present yourself more successfully to a potential employer. So challenge yourself to choose a format that works best for you—even if it looks different from what you've used or seen before.

Career Champ Profile: Jim

Jim had experienced many successes in his professional life, including starting and selling two businesses. Following his last business sale, Jim had gone to work as a consultant for the people who had bought Greenlands Grounds Maintenance Service, and he quickly skyrocketed to the top sales position in the region. But now he was ready for his next challenge. Jim wanted to secure a position as general manager with a company that needed a strong leader to raise it to the next level of success.

When we talked about which format to choose for his resume, organizing information chronologically just didn't seem to be the right choice. Jim hadn't necessarily progressed in one line of work; he'd worked in several different roles. And a functional format didn't seem quite right, either, because while Jim might choose to change into a different industry, he wanted to move back into a GM role.

"Let's try a hybrid format, just to see how it looks," I suggested. In the end, we came up with the following resume, which allowed Jim the flexibility to use just the first page, or both pages, to support his networking and job searching.

Jim Hollister *General Manager*

818 Green Leaf Drive
Fort Lupton, CO 80545
(970) 333-5959, jholl@email.com

Exceptional Goal-Driven Leader

Accomplished, experienced **General Manager** with proven track record for achieving impressive growth, maintaining long-term satisfied customers, and cultivating loyal, motivated teams; demonstrated strengths in coordinating sales, service, administration, and staff resulting in exceptional service and healthy profits; adept at preparing budgets, interpreting P&L statements, managing cash flow, and implementing ongoing operational improvements; able to inspire sales teams to achieve revenue growth goals and motivate administrative staff to operational excellence; skilled in ensuring compliance with regulations and processes; computer literate; highly personable.

WORK HISTORY & RELATED ACCOMPLISHMENTS

➢ **Consultant,** Gro-Right Landscape Services, 2005–Present
➢ **General Manager / Owner,** Greenlands Grounds Maintenance Service, 1999–2005
➢ **Software Trainer,** First Money Bank, 1998–1999
➢ **Account Manager,** TeleSTAFF / AA Temps, Inc., 1995–1998
➢ **General Manager / Owner,** Cat-n-Dog Junction, 1994–1995

_____*Selected Accomplishments*_____

Challenge / Opportunity	Action	Results
To grow a profitable, successful business.	Defined target clientele; networked for business; established procedures; developed teams; ensured consistent, quality service.	**Grew first-year revenues of $250k to $1.2 million within six years; earned premier-provider reputation in Northern Colorado.**
Respond to massive demand for service in response to blizzard of 2001.	Obtained additional equipment, organized 200+ operators, planned service routes, monitored results.	**Achieved successful service delivery 4 days ahead of competition.**
Ensure outstanding service and long-term customer loyalty.	Developed effective service-tracking and response process.	**Consistently responded to customer needs within 24 hours, resulting in referrals and growth.**

General Management Expertise..

• Proven track record for growing and managing operations exceeding $1.2 million in annual revenues, and effectively leading teams of 200+.
• Offer an outstanding ability to define and implement processes, schedules, and product offerings that ensure quality and ongoing profitability and growth.
• Adept at computer tools including Microsoft Office (Word, Excel, PowerPoint, Publisher), Quickbooks, ACT, JavaScript, and Blackberry.

EDUCATION
B.S. Agriculture & Biology, *General Business Minor*
Stephen F. Austin State University, *cum laude*

Detailed Work History on Following Page...

Figure 10.1: Jim's resume.

Jim Hollister   *General Manager*

Resume Page 2 of 2
(970) 333-5959, jholl@email.com

Exceptional Goal-Driven Leader

EXPANDED WORK HISTORY

Consultant, Gro-Right Landscape Services, 2005–Present
- Identify client prospects and establish relationships through networking and referrals.
- Consistently achieve top-sales-producer status for new business growth.
- Ensure client satisfaction through exceptional service delivery and problem solving.
- Support business with operational and business efficiency analyses to improve business performance.

General Manager / Owner, Greenlands Grounds Maintenance Service, 1999–2005
- Grew business to $1.2 million in annual revenues through effective leadership, quality service delivery, and establishment of excellent operational processes.
- Routinely conducted business efficiency analyses to improve effectiveness and profitability.
- Built high-performing teams of 200+ through successful recruiting, training, and leadership.
- Achieved outstanding fiscal results through effective P&L and accounting-process monitoring, including troubleshooting problems early to avoid larger problems.
- Eventually sold the business to CoCal Landscaping Services.

Software Trainer, First Money Bank, 1998–1999
- Developed and implemented computer technology training classes to a highly diverse, multicultural team of 2,000+ employees.
- Supported newly trained team members through help-desk support.
- Maintained cutting-edge knowledge of technology tools through ongoing learning.

Account Manager, TeleSTAFF / AA Temps, 1995–1998
- Successfully developed large-region sales territory through prospecting and excellent service.
- Planned and implemented effective marketing strategies leading to ongoing business growth.
- Used technology tools to improve operational efficiencies and maintain quality.
- Developed excellent employee screening and recruiting skills.

General Manager / Owner, Cat-n-Dog Junction, 1994–1995
- Identified need in the market, developed business plan, secured SBA financing, and achieved impressive first-year results.
- Secured 100+ customers, and built team of 5 well-trained service providers.
- Sold business to pursue other professional goals.

Possess additional work experience in retail store management and conference planning.
Details on request.

Background also includes international work experience in Brussels, and extensive travel in Germany, France, England, Scotland, Holland, Luxembourg, Italy, Switzerland, Austria, Canada, and Mexico.

Core Courage Concept

You're moving down the road toward creating an effective resume one successful step at a time: You chose an objective for your resume, created lists of keywords and key skill areas, made a first cut at some information to include in your document, developed your Work History and Education sections, selected some potential "extras" to include, and now you're deciding how you'll format all this great information. If all this work feels new and scary to you…it should! Chances are, you're creating your resume very differently than you ever have before, and you may worry about how things will turn out. But my guess is that deep down, you know you're on your way toward creating what will most likely turn out to be the best resume you've ever had…one baby step at a time.

Confidence Checklist

☐ Learn a little about different resume formats.

☐ Take a quick quiz to see which format will work best.

☐ Interpret your results and make your decision.

Chapter 11

Create a Compelling Chronological Resume

You've determined that a chronological resume is the ideal format to help you advance in your career. Now you'll build off the hard work you've done so far, making effective use of your Career Target, Keywords, Work History, and Education sections. Completion of your chronological resume is just minutes away, so let's get started!

Risk It or Run From It?

- **Risk Rating:** About as risky as putting together a slightly difficult puzzle: Not too big a deal, but it might challenge your brain a little.

- **Payoff Potential:** When you put these pieces together, you're going to feel great! Plus, your resume will be an effective tool to help you move forward in your career.

- **Time to Complete:** For the first draft, 30 minutes to an hour.

- **Bailout Strategy:** Talk someone else into doing it for you. Otherwise, you're going to have to build the first draft of your resume sometime…so why not now?

(continued)

(continued)

- **The "20 Percent Extra" Edge:** A well-organized, targeted resume will help land you on the short list from among the throng of other job searchers who have submitted their resumes.

- **"Go for It!" Bonus Activity:** After you've completed your chronological resume, send it out to several of your supporters, along with a list of companies that interest you, and ask for suggestions of people at those organizations to connect with regarding your job search. Their contacts will help you expand your job search network while quickly boosting your results.

How to Put Together Your Chronological Resume

In chapter 10, you completed a short questionnaire to help you decide which resume format will work best for you. If you're reading this chapter, you determined that you're either aiming to stay in the same line of work—targeting a position similar to the one you held most recently—or moving up to the next step within your chosen career. Because of your career goals, it makes sense to organize your resume chronologically. Now I'll walk you through a step-by-step process for putting together the first draft of this document.

Fill in the Basic Pieces of Your Chronological Resume

You'll be happy to know that you've already done much of the legwork for this resume (go ahead and feel a little smug for a few seconds if you want—you've earned it!). Now all your hard work will begin to pay off. Pull out the rough professional history you wrote in chapter 3, the header/objective/keyword block you created in chapter 5, the Work History outline you developed in chapter 7, the Education section you composed in chapter 8, as well as with any "extras" you listed in chapter 9. Now you'll plug them into your chronological resume.

The basic outline for your document will follow this order:

- Header/Objective/Keyword block

- Work History

- Education

The extras will fit in here and there as they make sense.

To begin building your actual resume, open a word processing file and enter the information you've already created. Your file will look something like figure 11.1.

AMANDA CLAIR
2001 Scenic Drive
Colorado Springs, CO 80638
(720) 288-8888, aclair@yahoo.com

Qualified, accomplished Psychotherapist with a proven track record for providing effective client support; possess strengths in clinical interviews, developing staffing plans, managing cases, and conducting individual, family, and group therapy; adept at case documentation, compliance with care standards, and facilitating client transitions; skilled in collaborating with other departments and agencies to implement effective treatments; offer strengths in dealing decisively with practical matters and crisis situations.

WORK HISTORY

➤ CAC I Certification Candidate (in progress), *State of Colorado*, 2007–Present
➤ On-call therapist, *Oak Behavioral Hospital,* 2004–2007
➤ Graduate Intern, *Outpatient & Residential Units, Oak Behavioral Hospital,* 2003–2004
➤ Domestic Violence Advocate, *Center for the Prevention of Domestic Violence,* 2001–2003

EDUCATION & CREDENTIALS

- M.A. Community Counseling, University of Northern Colorado
- B.A. Psychology, University of Colorado, Colorado Springs
- CAC I Certification, *anticipated completion 2008*
- CAC II & III Certifications, *in progress*

Figure 11.1: The basic pieces of the resume.

Don't worry if yours looks a little rougher than this example. As long as you have your header, objective, keyword statements, work history, and education information somewhere in the document, you're in good shape for now. You'll have plenty of chances to make improvements, add more content, and work on the formatting as we go along.

Expand Your Work Experience Section

As you've most likely seen in other chronological resumes (see examples on pages 41, 98, and 132), this format typically includes a description of the responsibilities held in each position. Sometimes it also includes information about the employer, and in some cases, details of your accomplishments on the job. The following steps will lead you through a process for adding these valuable details to your work history listings.

Begin with your most recent position and jot down a few notes about what the company did, as well as your responsibilities, tasks, and any accomplishments.

Panic Point! Writing down job responsibilities, a description of the company, and other data about a position frequently makes Career Cowards sweat. I'll confess...me too! (and I've written thousands of resumes). Because there are so many options for deciding what to include, the task can seem overwhelming. However, there are doable steps you can follow to effectively build this section, so keep on plugging!

To develop a sentence or two about the description of the company, fill in some basic information based on what you know about it. Or, if you want to get more formal, pull up the company's Web page or enter the company name on a search engine to find a few sentences describing the organization. Here's a sample sentence to help you start:

> "This organization developed/sold/provided support for X, Y, and Z."

If you want, you can add in some additional details, such as annual revenues, a specific department you worked in, and so on. But basically, one or two sentences about the company will be sufficient.

In Amanda's case, she's currently studying to pass a certification exam. While it's not technically a "job," she's working at this task to move forward in her career, so we're including it in her work history:

- CAC I Certification Candidate (in progress), *State of Colorado,* 2007–Present

To identify a few lines about the "company" (in this case, the certification division of the state), we conducted a search on www.google.com using the keywords "CAC I Certification State of Colorado" and came up with this line:

- Program developed to prepare counselors to become substance abuse treatment professionals.

Next, we needed to come up with a few lines describing Amanda's responsibilities.

Tip: For this step, it helps to stay focused on the key skill areas you prioritized in chapter 6, allowing you to create job description statements that highlight those abilities.

Because Amanda wanted to emphasize her counseling skills, training, and expertise working with a variety of mental health issues, we created a few statements related to these areas. We were able to find content to help describe her work on the Internet, looking through the same CAC I listing, and built the following description for the first listing in Amanda's Work History section.

CAC I Certification Candidate (*in progress*), <u>State of Colorado</u>, 2007–Present
Certification program to prepare counselors to become substance abuse treatment professionals.

- Currently building knowledge, skills, training, and work experience in the treatment of substance abuse issues.
- Gaining hands-on experience in Addictions Counseling Skills, Client Record Management, Principles of Addiction Treatment, Ethical Issues in Counseling, Infectious Diseases in the Substance Abuse population, Diversity Issues
- Completing 1,000 hours of work/field experience, supervised by a CACIII credentialed supervisor.

As you add details to your own Work History section, these resources may be helpful to you:

- **Your job description:** Do you (or the company's HR department) have a document detailing your position? That description may provide you some verbiage.

- **Job descriptions off a job search Web site:** Remember the process you went through in chapter 5, reviewing sample job descriptions off the Internet? Those same job descriptions can be an excellent resource to help you create position description statements. Find a few that describe the work you performed and then modify them to make them accurate for you.

- **The following "Sentence Starter" tool:** A listing of several action verbs helpful for beginning and writing your job description statements.

Sentence Starters

Begin statements in your resume with these "Sentence Starter" action words.

Achieved	Consulted	Diagnosed
Administered	Contributed	Drafted
Arranged	Coached	Delivered
Analyzed	Coordinated	Evaluated
Assessed	Counseled	Examined
Attained	Collected	Encouraged
Advised	Conceived	Eliminated
Assembled	Contracted	Excelled
Appraised	Decided	Expanded
Authored	Defined	Estimated
Budgeted	Detailed	Formulated
Built	Developed	Formed
Calculated	Distributed	Facilitated

Founded	Negotiated	Scheduled
Generated	Participated	Sold
Guided	Performed	Simplified
Gathered	Problem solved	Structured
Gained	Persuaded	Surveyed
Handled	Promoted	Screened
Helped	Purchased	Supervised
Implemented	Planned	Summarized
Improved	Programmed	Translated
Investigated	Recruited	Transformed
Introduced	Revitalized	Tailored
Investigated	Referred	Trained
Installed	Reviewed	Tested
Launched	Researched	Upgraded
Maintained	Repaired	Validated
Mastered	Remodeled	Verified
Motivated	Reported	Visualized
Managed	Recommended	Verbalized
Mentored	Recruited	Volunteered
Monitored	Searched	Wrote

- **Web sites:** Sites such as www.careerinfonet.org provide comprehensive descriptions of many occupations.

After you've written a few bullets (somewhere between three to five statements is usually enough) describing the key aspects of your position, call it "good enough!" Then move on to your next most recent position in your work history, following the same process to develop an expanded job description. Repeat this process until you've filled in details for as many positions as you're choosing to include.

> **Tip:** Be careful not to get caught in "paralysis by analysis"—a situation in which you keep rewording your work experience descriptions, trying to make them perfect, and wind up getting stuck! Later in this book we'll do some final editing and finishing, spending a little more time improving your descriptions. But for now, get some details on paper and then move on to the next step.

Add in "Extras" and Other Details

Now you can plug in a few of the extras you may have identified in chapter 9. Extras can quickly move your resume from being "good" to being "great!" So, which accomplishments might you include? Do you have any awards or associations worth mentioning?

> **Panic Point!** Career Cowards are often nervous about including extras that are too self-promoting. They worry about coming across as "braggy" and tooting their own horn too strongly. However, it's been my experience that including extras can result in huge improvements in the results your resume generates. And as long as you're presenting factual information, you're not bragging! In the end, you may decide *not* to include extras, and that's okay. But for now, if you have an achievement or some other extra you're considering including, put it in. You can always take it out later.

And then (drum roll, please), congratulations! You've created the first draft of your chronological resume! In chapter 14, you'll have the chance to make final changes and add finishing touches, but for now, celebrate what you've created so far.

Why It's Worth Doing

A well-written and organized chronological resume provides potential employers with a quick, informative overview of your career progression within a specific field. Composing job descriptions that not only describe your experience but emphasize your expertise in key skill areas helps you paint an effective picture of your capabilities for the resume screener. Your chronological resume will blend the best of what you've accomplished in your career so far with where you're headed!

Career Champ Profile: Amanda

Amanda loved her work as a counselor and was taking concrete steps to grow in her career. She needed a resume that would reflect the steady progress she was making professionally, so she decided that a chronological format would be the best choice for her.

In the following example, Amanda lists her self-study activities as a component of her work history, allowing her to highlight her focus on continuing career advancement, while also filling in a gap in her timeline. She also plugged in a few "extras"—accomplishments as well as an association membership—to build her credibility and make her resume even more interesting.

Core Courage Concept

Putting together a resume can be tough, especially when it comes to describing what you did in your former positions. Yet you're committed to pushing through even the tough steps to accomplish your career goals. Take a look at what you've created to this point. Even though this task has probably felt new and a little scary, you're doing it! Take a deep breath now because you've definitely completed the toughest parts of this process. The rest is pretty easy. Congratulations!

AMANDA CLAIR
2001 Scenic Drive
Colorado Springs, CO 80638
(720) 288-8888, aclair@yahoo.com

Qualified, accomplished Psychotherapist with a proven track record for providing effective client support; possess strengths in clinical interviews, developing staffing plans, managing cases, and conducting individual, family, and group therapy; adept at case documentation, compliance with care standards, and facilitating client transitions; skilled in collaborating with other departments and agencies to implement effective treatments; offer strengths in dealing decisively with practical matters and crisis situations.

WORK HISTORY

CAC I Certification Candidate (in progress), State of Colorado, 2007–Present
Certification program to prepare counselors to become substance abuse treatment professionals.
- Currently building knowledge, skills, training, and work experience in the treatment of substance abuse issues.
- Gaining hands-on experience in Addictions Counseling Skills, Client Record Management, Principles of Addiction Treatment, Ethical Issues in Counseling, Infectious Diseases in the Substance Abuse population, Diversity.
- Completing 1,000 hours of field experience, supervised by a CACIII credentialed supervisor.

Psychotherapist, Private Practice, 2004–2006
Counseling practice supporting individuals and families.
- Supported individuals and families through diagnosis of mental illness, development of treatment plans, and maintenance of client records.
- Provided community education programs on mental health issues:
  ✓ **Developed and conducted Domestic Violence Workshops for college students.**

On-call therapist, Cedar Grove Behavioral Hospital, 2004–2005....................................
Graduate Intern, 2003–2004
Mental health facility serving local community.
- Handled intake, assessment, crisis intervention, discharge planning, and insurance compliance.
- Conducted individual, group, and family sessions for child, adolescent, and adult crisis units.
- Worked effectively with diverse teams and coordinated treatment with staff members.
- *Selected Accomplishments:*
  ✓ **Transformed existing DUI workshop materials into interesting creative group sessions for court-ordered clients.**
  ✓ **Served as patient advocate with insurance companies to gain approval for care.**
- Conducted tests relevant to drug dependence, supported clients in quest to be free of chemical dependence, and motivated clients to stay in treatment.
- Built productive relationships with support agencies, new clients, and hospital departments.

EDUCATION, CREDENTIALS & ASSOCIATIONS

- **M.A. Community Counseling,** University of Northern Colorado
- **B.A. Psychology,** University of Colorado, Colorado Springs
- **CAC I Certification,** *completion August 2008*
- **Member, American Counseling Association**

Figure 11.2: Amanda's resume.

Confidence Checklist

☐ Fill in the basic pieces of your chronological resume.

☐ Expand your Work Experience section.

☐ Add in "extras" and other details.

Chapter 12

Format a Fantastic Functional Resume

Based on your personal situation, you've determined that a resume formatted in a functional style will work best to help you achieve your career goals. In this chapter, I lead you through an easy-to-execute process for pulling together a document that allows you to emphasize the most relevant aspects of your background, using a highly effective resume-building approach.

Risk It or Run From It?

- **Risk Rating:** This is a mid-range risk activity. If you've never written a resume in this format before, it may feel a little strange.

- **Payoff Potential:** Outstanding! If you're changing careers, have little experience, are fresh out of school, or are filling in a gap in your work history, this format can work wonders for you.

- **Time to Complete:** About an hour.

- **Bailout Strategy:** Have someone else do it for you. (Pssst....know what, though? It's really not that difficult, and when you see how it works, it's fun and very rewarding. Why not give it a try?)

(continued)

(continued)

- **The "20 Percent Extra" Edge:** A fantastic functional resume can transform who you are in the eyes of decision makers or resume screeners. It's truly one of the most amazing career tools at your disposal.

- **"Go for It!" Bonus Activity:** Once you've finished your newly created functional resume, have a little fun with it by showing it to a few of your supporters for just 10 seconds per person. After they've looked at it for that short period of time, ask them to make their best guess about the career target for which you're planning. If you've done your job well, they'll be able to identify your career goal and qualifications instantly!

How to Build Your Functional Resume

You've decided that for you a functional resume format is the best choice. In the short questionnaire you completed in chapter 10, you answered "yes" to "I am entering a brand-new career field, either as a career changer or as a recent graduate just beginning in my profession" or "I haven't been in the workforce in the last number of years—either because I was a student, or because I took off time from work to raise children, handle an illness, care for a family member, or for some other reason." Now you'll pull together the pieces you've developed so far into a complete and effective functional resume.

Plug in the Resume Pieces You've Already Created

All the hard work you've done in the preceding chapters will begin to pay off now. So pull out the rough professional history you wrote up in chapter 3, the header/objective/keyword block you created in chapter 5, the key skill areas you prioritized in chapter 6, the Work History outline you developed in chapter 7, the Education section you composed in chapter 8, as well as with any extras you listed in chapter 9. You'll be using them as you develop your functional resume.

The basic outline for your document will roughly follow this order:

- Header/Objective/Keyword block

- Work History listing

- Key Skill Areas Expertise section

- Education

Or, if you're a fresh graduate of a training program, it may make sense for you to swap the Education and Work History sections in your document, allowing you to emphasize the training you recently acquired. Your resume outline would then follow this order:

- Header/Objective/Keyword block

- Education

- Key Skill Areas Expertise section

- Work History listing

The extras will fit in here and there as they make sense.

Figure 12.1 is an example of these sections for Maury, a job searcher who had spent the last decade as an at-home parent, aiming to find work as an office administrator.

Don't sweat it if your Header, Keyword Block, Work History, and Education sections aren't as nicely laid out as this example. For now, we're just plugging in the pieces. Later, you'll have the chance to improve the formatting.

Maury Claudell
2831 Cherry Hills Drive
Fort Collins, CO 80525
(970) 222-7777 mgclaudell@comcast.net

Effective Office Support professional with excellent communication, organization, and dependability skills; possess 5+ years of office administration background, with proficiency in Microsoft Word, Excel, and the Internet; offer excellent customer service abilities, with strengths in prioritizing and handling multiple tasks in a fast-paced environment.

WORK HISTORY

• Support Specialist	Platte School District	2006–Present
• At-Home Parent		2005
• Service Manager	Craft World	2003–2004
• At-Home Parent		1998–2003
• Office & Operations Manager	Blackwell & Company, Inc.	1995–1998

KEY SKILL AREAS

Office Administration, Computer Skills & Organization
Communication & Customer Support

EDUCATION

Bachelor of Science Degree in Business Administration, University of Northern Colorado

Figure 12.1: "Extra" sections for Maury.

Develop Content for Your Key Skill Area Sections

Remember back in chapter 6, when I walked you through identifying the key skill areas for your career target? Pull those out now. They're an essential piece of an effective functional resume.

Maury's career target is an office administration position. After reviewing a few sample job descriptions and boiling those down to the most important responsibilities, she determined that the top key skill areas for the position were

- Office Support Background

- Computer Skills

- Customer Service Experience

Panic Point! Career Cowards frequently have a little freak-out session when it comes to choosing key skill areas. "What if I don't choose the *right* ones?" they worry. First of all, keep in mind that there are no *right ones*. You're just using your best judgment. I find it's best to pick three or so key skill areas that at that moment seem to be good choices, and work with them as I develop the rest of the functional resume. Later, I may discover that they just aren't working out—perhaps they're too similar to each other or really don't emphasize the expertise I'm aiming for—so I end up changing them. So try not to get too worried about choosing the "right ones." Just pick a few, start writing, and modify them later if you need to. Once you've decided on your key skill areas (at least your first-best-guess at them!), write them down on a pad of paper or enter them in a word processing file. You'll need them for the next step.

Brainstorm Your Expertise Related to Your Key Skill Areas

From here, you're going to build the most important component of a functional resume: the Key Skill Area Expertise section. As you look at the examples of functional resumes on pages 30, 59, and 70, you'll see that each includes a large section of content providing specific experience statements related to the key skill areas. That's the part that you're going to create for yourself right now.

To begin, choose one of the key skill areas on your list. Then ask yourself, "When have I demonstrated my expertise with this particular skill?" Remember that your experiences may come from a variety of sources:

- A former job

- A class or study program (self-study counts, too!)

- Volunteer work

- Practice projects you've completed on your own

It's also helpful to review the "master closet" of experiences you created in chapter 3. As you brainstorm instances related to one of your key skill areas, keep an open mind about where you may have acquired those experiences. As a recruiter once told me, "I don't care where someone obtained their expertise—whether it was on a job, through volunteering, or whatever—it counts!"

Additionally (and this is one of the greatest advantages of using a functional format), you can draw on experiences from any time in your life—even if it was many, many years ago. So if you catch yourself thinking, "Well, I did use that skill 20 years ago, but isn't that too old?" write it down anyway.

Do your best to write down several examples of times when you've demonstrated your expertise with a particular skill. For ideas, it may help to review the rough draft of the professional history you created in chapter 3. Looking over the sample job descriptions you gathered in chapters 4 and 5 and asking yourself "When have I done these kinds of things?" may also be useful for this step. The more instances of your experiences you can brainstorm, the more possibilities you have to work with on your resume.

Panic Point! "I don't have much (if any) experience with a particular key skill area. How do I handle that?" This is a common reaction for many Career Cowards as they begin to build their Key Skills Experience section. The worry is that you won't have enough evidence to qualify you for your career target. However, I've discovered after interviewing thousands of job searchers about their backgrounds that *you can almost always come up with some experience related to a particular key skill area.* Although you may not think your experience is "good enough," chances are, it's probably fine. So give yourself the benefit of the doubt and challenge yourself to write down anything that comes to mind...even if you worry that it's not "good enough."

Push yourself to brainstorm at least three to five examples of times when you've used or learned about a particular skill. These were the examples Maury came up with:

Office Support Background

- I once successfully managed day-to-day office operations for 6 years, providing support to a team of financial advisors.

- In this job, I implemented and followed through on administrative procedures, ensuring that everyone had adequate resources and supplies, and resolving problems in the office.

- Also, I input and maintained thousands of account and financial details over several years with an excellent record for accuracy.

- Additionally, I've helped out at my husband's office many times, answering phones, filing, chipping in wherever I was needed.

Computer and Office Equipment Skills

- I am familiar with a broad range of office technology: multiline phones, fax machines and copiers, computers and software, including Microsoft Office and the Internet.

- Helping out at my children's school, I used to assist the teachers with data entry tasks on their computers.

- At school, I also operated copiers and other equipment.

- We have a computer at home, and I use it to keep track of our family's expenses using Quicken. I also create letters and small desktop publishing projects.

Customer Service Experience

- My background includes 5+ years in customer service roles, working both at Blackwell and Craft World.

- At Blackwell, I worked with diverse customer personalities, managing and responding to thousands of customer service details.

- In this position, I kept a detailed database of contacts, deadlines, daily checklists, phone numbers, menu selections, hotel accommodations, and other detailed client information in order to respond to client needs.

- At Craft World, service was the biggest part of my job. I helped customers find what they were looking for, answered questions about how certain products worked, and solved problems.

Using this information, as well as terminology and phrasing she found in some of her sample job descriptions, Maury was able to prioritize which pieces of information would be best to include, and to develop the main content statements for the Key Skills Experience section of her resume. She then added in some "extras" to finish up the section.

Add in "Extras" and Other Details

Remember the "extras" you developed in chapter 9? This is a good time to pull those out and decide which you may want to include in your resume. A few well-placed achievements, awards, and associations can greatly improve the impact of your functional resume.

Then—guess what? You've just finished building the first draft of your functional resume! In chapter 14, you'll have the chance to make final changes and add finishing touches, but for now, celebrate what you've created so far. Congratulations!

Why It's Worth Doing

A well-structured functional resume can help you effectively communicate where you're going in your career, as compared to a chronological resume, which puts the emphasis on the step-by-step progression of your career to this point. So if you've been involved in different endeavors prior to now, this format can be a huge asset for you because it allows you to highlight the pieces of your background that are especially relevant to your career target, in a format that's clear, attractive, and effective.

"Does this format really work? It looks pretty weird to me!" you may be thinking. You're not the first person to question the effectiveness of a functional resume. Yet having witnessed the results of thousands of job searchers who used a functional resume, I can say with confidence, it *definitely* works! But I realize that you may not believe me until you try it and see for yourself. So give it a go and let me know how it works for you!

Career Champ Profile: Maury

After finishing college, Maury launched into a career as a fast-paced office administrator in the financial world. Then, a few years later, she got married and devoted several years of her life to raising two wonderful children. When she was ready to get back into the workforce, she needed a resume that would play up her skills and experience, while playing down the gaps in her work history. This is what we put together:

Maury Claudell   *Administrative/ Office Manager*
2831 Cherry Hills Drive
Fort Collins, CO 80525
(970) 222-7777 mgclaudell@comcast.net

Effective office support professional with excellent communication, organization, and dependability skills; possess 5+ years of office administration background, with proficiency in Microsoft Word, Excel, and the Internet; offer excellent customer service abilities, with strengths in prioritizing and handling multiple tasks in a fast-paced environment.

WORK HISTORY & RELATED EXPERIENCE

➢ **Support Specialist**	Platte School District	2006–Present
➢ **At-Home Parent**		2005
➢ **Service Manager**	Craft World	2003–2004
➢ **At-Home Parent**		1998–2003
➢ **Office Manager**	Blackwell & Company, Inc.	1995–1998

Office Administration, Computer Skills & Organization

- Successfully managed day-to-day office operations for 6 years, providing support to team specialists, implementing and following through on administrative procedures, ensuring adequate resources and supplies, and resolving office issues.
- Offer outstanding organization and attention-to-detail skills.
  - ✓ **Input and maintained thousands of account and financial details over several years with an excellent record for accuracy.**
- Able to effectively use a broad range of office technology: multiline phones, fax machines and copiers, computers and software: MS Office, Internet, etc.

Expertise in Communication & Customer Support

- Personable and professional, with a proven ability to maintain calm and a sense of humor in busy office environments.
- Background includes 5+ years in customer care roles, establishing effective working relationships, collecting and responding to critical information, and maintaining client data.
- Worked with diverse customer personalities in brokerage industry, managing and responding to thousands of customer service details.
  - ✓ **Operated a highly organized and successful customer care operation, and regularly received kudos for accuracy and professionalism.**
- Expert in responding to and managing phone requests, orders, and reservations.
  - ✓ *Example:* Kept a detailed database of contacts, deadlines, daily checklists, phone numbers, menu selections, hotel accommodations, and other detailed client information in order to respond to client needs in brokerage support position.

EDUCATION

Bachelor of Science Degree in Business Administration with emphasis in
Office Systems Management from the University of Northern Colorado, Greeley, Colorado

Figure 12.2: Maury's resume.

Core Courage Concept

If you've never used a functional resume format (yet, because of your situation it makes sense to…), allowing yourself to build and use a resume organized in this way can feel weird and probably a little unsettling. But chances are very good that if you're reading this book, you're an open-minded person looking for *new* ways to put together a resume that helps you achieve your career goals. Even though this format may look a little strange to you, you've created a functionally formatted resume, and now you're going to finalize it and see how it works. Good for you! I predict that you'll be very pleased with the career doors this approach can open for you.

Confidence Checklist

- ☐ Plug in the resume pieces you've already created.
- ☐ Brainstorm your expertise related to your key skill areas.
- ☐ Add in "extras" and other details.

Chapter 13

Produce a Powerful Hybrid or Curriculum Vitae Style Resume

When traditional and functional resume formats don't meet your career needs, then a hybrid or curriculum vitae (CV) style may be just right for you. The resume development work you've done to this point can be put to good use now, as you combine your Career Focus, Keywords, Work History, and Education sections into a unique document that allows you to move toward achievement of your career objectives.

Risk It or Run From It?

- **Risk Rating:** Low to mid-range risk. You're just going to experiment with a few other resume formats.

- **Payoff Potential:** If the hybrid or curriculum vitae (CV) resume format is the best choice for you, using one of these organizational methods will allow you to present your information effectively, leading to big career payoffs.

- **Time to Complete:** An hour or so.

(continued)

(continued)

- **Bailout Strategy:** Stick with one of the other formats (chronological or functional) or hire someone to create your hybrid resume or CV for you.

- **The "20 Percent Extra" Edge:** Just as having the right tool can make a huge difference in completing a certain task, using the best resume format for your situation can make a huge difference in your results. A hybrid or CV format may be the "right tool" you need!

- **"Go for It!" Bonus Activity:** Conduct a search on the Internet for additional examples of hybrid and CV style resumes. There are many ways to format these documents, and looking at a range of examples will help you determine the approach that works best for you.

How to Build Your Hybrid or Curriculum Vitae Resume

In chapter 10, you determined that either a hybrid or CV resume format made the most sense for you. In this chapter, I walk you through the process of developing resumes in both of these formats.

Create a Chronological Resume as Your First Step Toward Developing Your Hybrid Resume

When you completed the short questionnaire in chapter 10, your "yes" answer to either "I work (or did work) for the same company for more than 10 years and have held multiple positions within that company. The next step I'm targeting in my career will be toward one of those types of positions" or "My career situation is truly unique" led to your decision to create a hybrid format resume. This resume format is a combination of both the chronological and functional resume formats, so I'll refer you to chapters 11 and 12 as part of the process for creating your document.

Because a hybrid resume is basically a chronological resume with the addition of a few functional formatting elements, you can begin by reading and following the steps described in chapter 11 to create a chronological resume. This will provide you with the foundation for your hybrid resume.

Add in Functional Resume Elements Where They Make Sense

Now you can add in functional resume elements to highlight certain skills in your background. Because there are many ways to add in functional sections to your hybrid resume, keep an open mind about what will work best for you. For instance, check out the Career Champ resume example in chapter 10. See how Jim included information that was organized both functionally and chronologically? And in the example for Cory in the appendix, you'll notice that Cory included a listing of "Sample Engineering & Design Projects" as a way to highlight his skills in engineering.

To get ideas for how you might want to enhance the basic chronological resume you developed, read through chapter 12, keeping in mind the following suggestions:

- The purpose for adding in a functional section is to *highlight skills in your background that are especially important to resume screeners*. As you decide which functional sections to add, be sure to keep your focus on the top priority skill areas.

- At the most, emphasize only one to three key skill areas in your hybrid resume. Otherwise, your document can end up looking confusing and long (for more suggestions on ideal length, see chapter 14). Keep in mind that most resume screeners aren't interested in slogging through a resume that goes on and on. Focus on your priorities and keep your hybrid resume to the point.

- Experiment with how and where you add in functional elements. There are many ways to present the information, so check out various ideas presented in this book.

Panic Point! Career Cowards often worry that the guidelines for building a hybrid resume format seem too "loose" and want a more orderly, step-by-step process to follow. It's very important to keep reminding yourself that there's *no single "right" way to write a resume!* When you find yourself panicking over how to format your information, take a deep breath and tell yourself, "I'll play with some formatting ideas for now and eventually find one that I like." And guess what...you will!

Pull Together the Key Pieces of Your Information for Your Curriculum Vitae

If you're targeting a position as a teacher, professor, or administrator in academia, then a CV format may be the best choice for you. In my experience, a CV is one of the easiest types of resumes to develop because it's primarily made up of category listings and is more straightforward than other resume formats.

To begin building your CV, pull out the following pieces of information:

- The rough professional history you wrote in chapter 3

- The header/objective/keyword block you created in chapter 5

- The Work History outline you developed in chapter 7

- The Education section you composed in chapter 8

- The "extras" you listed in chapter 9

The information included in a CV can be presented in many ways, but often the organization follows this order:

- Header

- Education

- Work History

- Research projects

- Publications

- Presentations

- Affiliations

Check out the Career Champ example in this chapter to see an abbreviated version of a CV, keeping in mind that often CVs are several pages long (I once worked on a CV for a math professor that was 14 pages long!). You can also find even more CV ideas by entering the keywords "CV samples" to locate several examples on the Internet.

Why It's Worth Doing

Sometimes the traditional approach to resumes just won't work for your situation. When a chronological format seems too "traditional" and a functional resume seems too "unusual," then a hybrid or CV format may be just right for you. Working through the steps to create a strong hybrid or CV resume can go a long way toward positioning you as the ideal candidate for good-fit career opportunities. Sometimes the road less traveled is just the right path!

Career Champ Profile: Sallie

Sallie is about to complete her doctorate and is thinking ahead to her next career goal: to line up a position heading a research lab at another university. We worked together to create the following CV for her. It's shown in an abbreviated version in figure 13.1.

Sallie Peterson

Department of Environmental and Radiological Health Sciences   (970) 555-3333
Colorado State University, Fort Collins, CO 80526   sallie.peterson@colostate.edu

EDUCATION

- **Ph.D., Radiological Health Sciences,** Colorado State University, *In Progress*
- **Doctor of Veterinary Medicine,** Colorado State University, 2005
- **Bachelor of Science, Agriculture Economics,** Duke University, 2000

PROFESSIONAL EXPERIENCE

Post-Doctoral Student/Ph.D. Candidate, 2005–Present
Department of Environmental and Radiological Health Sciences
Colorado State University, Fort Collins, CO

Veterinary Pathology Resident/Ph.D. Candidate, 2000–2005
Colorado State University, Fort Collins, CO

SEMINARS/TEACHING

Instructor, Department of Environmental and Radiological Health Sciences
Colorado State University, Fort Collins, CO
- Facilitated research progress, proposal, and informational seminars to Ph.D. students for fall and spring semesters.

PUBLICATIONS

- Peterson, S., Juarez, P.H., Tyson, R.E., Oates, K.G., Dalmer, Mortimer, R.G., & Dornstead, N.L. (2006). An economic model of prepartum nutrition and body condition score in poultry. *Colorado State University Poultry Program Report*, 111–114.

PROFESSIONAL LICENSURE/BOARD CERTIFICATION

- American College of Veterinary Pathologists, Board Eligible
- Colorado State Board License, Inactive, 2004–2006; Active, 2000–2004

PROFESSIONAL ASSOCIATIONS

- American Veterinary Medicine Association (AVMA), Active Member
- American Association for Cancer Research (AACR), Active Member
- Radiation Research Society, Member 2001–2004

AWARDS/SCHOLARSHIPS

- NIH Summer Fellowship Training Grant, 2005
- Pfizer Animal Health Veterinary Scholarship Award, 2000

Figure 13.1: Sallie's abbreviated CV.

Core Courage Concept

Chronological, functional, hybrid, or CV…which resume format will work best for you? The choices can seem confusing, yet you've taken the time to consider the advantages of each, and you've made a good choice for your situation—even though you may have felt unsure about your choice. Still, you persisted, and now you've built a document that will move you ahead toward achievement of your career goals. You've come a long way, and now you're in the home stretch. Kudos to you!

Confidence Checklist

- ☐ Create a chronological resume as your first step toward developing your hybrid resume.
- ☐ Add in functional resume elements where they make sense.
- ☐ Pull together the key pieces of your information for your curriculum vitae.

Chapter 14

Finalize Your Resume with Effective Formatting Techniques

Y ou're at the final step in the development of your fantastic resume. Take a few extra minutes now to enhance the formatting of your document, to make it the best it can be!

Risk It or Run From It?

- **Risk Rating:** Relatively low. You're just experimenting with ways to make a good thing even better.

- **Payoff Potential:** Great! The appearance of your resume, improved through effective formatting techniques, can boost its chances for being favorably noticed.

- **Time to Complete:** 15 to 30 minutes.

- **Bailout Strategy:** These formatting suggestions are optional. Although they will improve the look (and results) of your resume, you can skip them if you want.

- **The "20 Percent Extra" Edge:** The additional effort you put into making your resume look its best can have a huge impact on the number of interviews your resume generates.

(continued)

(continued)

> • **"Go for It!" Bonus Activity:** Stop by your local library or bookstore and flip through several resume sample books for additional formatting ideas.

How to Improve the Look of Your Resume

Thanks to the power of word processing, you can format the look of your resume in an infinite number of ways. With so many options, there are also as many opportunities to mess it up! The following information, providing formatting recommendations for both hard-copy and electronic resumes, will help ensure that your resume looks and performs its best.

Make Effective Font Choices

You've most likely scanned the long list of font choices available within your word processing program. With just the click of your mouse, you can transform the look of your font from conservative to modern to something unique. So which fonts does it make sense to choose? Following are guidelines to help with your selections:

- **Stick with a "mainstream" font.** Although you have the power to choose from many creative fonts, I strongly recommend selecting one that is widely used and visually "safe," such as Times New Roman, Arial, or Helvetica. Why limit yourself to just these few boring ones? Because (a) if you submit your resume electronically, resume screeners on the other end will most likely be able to successfully view that font on their computer (not all people have every font loaded on their computer, but almost all of them have the mainstream ones!), and (b) most of us see these fonts frequently enough that they've come to appear "normal" and acceptable—two traits that you want to convey with your resume! While you may think the Broadway font is just gorgeous, resume screeners may think, "Yuck! I hate this font, and therefore, probably won't like this person either." If you get too creative with your choice of fonts, you run the risk of eliciting a negative reaction from readers, as in "Yikes! This candidate seems weird!"

- **Use only one to two font types in your document.** Should you mix Times New Roman with Helvetica? Arial with Book Antiqua? Although I've seen many very beautiful resumes developed using multiple fonts, I suggest that you stick with one—or at the most, two—fonts. Unless you're a professional graphic artist (and if you are, see my comments further down regarding design and graphic elements), you run the risk of creating a document that looks like a three-ring circus, with too many things going on, and some of them pretty goofy! As you've probably noticed with the resume examples included in this book, I typically use only one font in the resumes I develop. Similar to my comment in the preceding guideline, it's "safer."

- **Be consistent in your use of font sizes.** I recommend that the text in your resume be produced using only one font size. For readability, I recommend using 12-, 11-, or 10.5-point text. Anything bigger can come across looking "clunky," and anything smaller will probably make your document difficult for screeners to read.

Panic Point! I know that sometimes there's a huge temptation to reduce the point size of your text so that you can squeeze in just one more great comment about you, *but resist that urge!* Never forget that resume screeners may be spending only a few seconds scanning your resume. If the text is too small, and if the document looks too "packed," you could quickly wind up in the "No, Thank You" pile because your resume is too much work to read. It's better to edit out some text than to reduce the point size.

Although I recommend using only one font size for the text part of your resume, I do think it's effective to use a larger font size for your name, section headings (such as "Work Experience" or "Education"), and job title to help readers quickly locate key pieces of information about you. Often, I'll use an 18-point size for the candidate's name and a 14-point size for the job title and section headings.

Work Within the Default Margins in Your Word Processing File

We've all seen documents in which the author reduced the margins to squeeze more on the page. Yet instead of achieving the goal of looking "capable," the author comes across as seeming wordy and unable to prioritize.

When I open a word processing file, my computer automatically sets my document margins at 1 inch at the top and bottom and 1.25 inches on the sides. Your settings are probably similar. I strongly recommend that you stick with the established margins and not "skinny" them down so that you can cram in more information. Your resume will look nicer, and its readability will be improved. Plus, you greatly reduce the risk of having a warning message pop up on the resume screener's computer about a problem with your margin sizes being outside the normal range—a little issue that may motivate the resume screener to think, "Never mind, I'll pass on this candidate."

Choose an Appropriate Resume Length

The hard-and-fast rule "Just one page!" doesn't necessarily hold true for resumes any more. Many resumes, especially those submitted electronically, may be far longer than what would fit on an 8½" × 11" page. That's okay, provided you take into account these other factors when deciding on the length of your resume:

- If you can communicate the most important information on one page, go for it. It's easier for screeners to handle and review.

- If describing your background takes more than one page, *be sure that all your content is relevant and concise.* One guideline is that if you have more than 10 years of experience in one career field, it's acceptable to have more than one page in your resume.

- Resumes will rarely exceed two (or at the most, three!) pages. Any longer than that, and you run a high risk of winding up in the "No, Thank You!" pile. Curriculum vitae are the exception to this rule. Often they will run three pages or longer.

If you find yourself struggling to fit all your information on a page or two, review chapter 4 to ensure that you've chosen a clear focus for your resume (unfocused resumes will frequently run on and on and on and on…) and chapter 6 to remind yourself of the key skill areas for your career target. Then evaluate all the information on your resume, asking yourself, "Is this piece of information really relevant?" Throw out anything that isn't.

Add Bolding, Underlines, and Italics to Emphasize Information

Bolding, underlining, and italicizing information will draw more attention to specific pieces of data in your resume. Please see the examples included in this book for ideas for using these treatments.

Highlight Your Position Objective Clearly

Keeping in mind that you may have only a few seconds of a resume screener's attention, it's essential to quickly communicate the position you're targeting. It's not unusual for a hiring coordinator to be recruiting for several positions at once. As a result, the easier you make it for resume screeners to understand what you're aiming for, the more likely you are to pass the initial screening process.

From my first career in advertising, I learned that readers will most often look at the upper-right corner of a document first. That's why, in several of the examples included in this book, we've positioned the job title in that location. Another effective technique is to list your job target directly underneath your header, near the top of the page. Wherever you choose to place your job target, be sure it stands out clearly.

Apply Graphic Elements Effectively

Used wisely, bullets, lines, and other graphic elements can quickly add sophistication while making your resume easier and more appealing to read. Looking through the examples in this book, you'll see that we've made creative use of bullets, boxes, lines, shading, drop caps, and even periods. These guidelines will help you determine how and when to use graphic elements:

- **Create sections in your resume using lines and shading to designate Work Experience, Education, and other sections.** You can add these elements by using the Borders and Shading feature in your word processing software or by typing periods in a row to create a line.

- **Use bullets to assist readers in locating key information about you.** As you remember, your resume may receive only a few seconds of a screener's attention. By bulleting statements rather than presenting them in longer paragraphs, you make it easier for readers to scan your information. However, avoid creating long "lists" of bullets (more than four in a row, which can look overwhelming to read) by breaking up the information with a different treatment. For instance, you can vary a long list of bullets by highlighting accomplishments with check marks or arrows and indenting them further on the page.

- **Add in a drop cap to give resume screeners a clear place to begin reading.** Drop caps—the enlarged first letter included on many of the resume examples in this book as well as on the first page of each chapter!—are a popular design element used to improve the appearance of a document while also giving readers clear direction about where to begin reading. Most word processing programs offer a drop cap feature. To find out how to use yours, enter **drop cap** in the Help window for more information.

- **Use boxes to highlight very important information.** Create a box around your Keyword section, for example, to quickly draw attention to your most important skills.

Panic Point! Career Cowards frequently sweat over the use of design elements. Although lines and bullets can greatly improve the look of your resume, be wary about including too many. Think of them as accessories used to enhance the overall appearance of your document. Just as you wouldn't wear three neckties or carry four handbags, don't go overboard by overusing a single design element. And unless you're aiming for a position in which visual creativity is an essential part of the job (such as graphic designer), err on the side of being more conservative rather than "unique."

Invest in Quality Resume Paper in a Neutral Color

I'm frequently asked, "Is it really worth the expense to buy fancy resume paper?" My answer is consistently "Yes!" A friend of mine who runs an employment service once described for me how nice it is to come across a resume printed on quality paper among the stacks of hundreds of resumes she handles each day. It immediately communicates to her that the candidate is worth considering. Any stock in the resume paper section of your local office supply store is adequate.

Regarding color, I strongly recommend sticking with a neutral white or cream. These colors are easiest to read, and if your resume ends up being photocopied, white and cream reproduce most success-fully. Seem boring? Would you rather choose a more interesting color? Keep in mind that the purpose of your resume is to get you in the door for an interview. While you may think Passion Purple is the way to go, resume screeners may hate it and quickly throw your resume in the "No Way!" pile. Yet it's rare to have a strong negative reaction to plain old white.

Use Photos Cautiously

Similar to the use of an unusual paper color, photos run the risk of turning off resume screeners. You don't want to unnecessarily elicit an "I don't like her striped scarf...she's outta here!" reaction. However, there are instances when a photo of yourself can help you stand out among your competition.

As an example, you can see that we've included a photo in Richard Springer's resume in chapter 9. He was aiming to enter the hunting and fishing industry, and his photo clearly communicated his enthusiasm for the job. I have also recommended including a photo in situations in which appearance and face-to-face interaction are important to the position, such as in sales or broadcasting.

If you decide to include a photo, be sure the quality is excellent. A professionally photographed headshot is usually your safest bet.

Format Your Resume as "Text Only" When Necessary

Although most resume screeners are capable of successfully opening and reading resumes produced in Microsoft Word, some hiring coordinators will ask you to submit your resume as a text file. In this case, you need to create two types of resume files: a version using the formatting features described throughout this book (this is the format you will use most often when applying electronically or when producing a paper copy of your resume), as well as a plain text version, to be submitted when a text file of your resume is requested.

To do this, you will need to save your document in a plain text format using the Save As feature in your word processing program. As your word processing program will warn you, saving your resume in a plain text format will remove most of the formatting you may have added to your document, such as borders, bolding, and even line breaks, making it much less readable. Therefore, you will need to add in some new formatting features *after* you've saved it as a text file. The Career Champ example in this chapter demonstrates the use of spacing, asterisks, periods, and dashes to improve readability in a plain text version of a resume.

Why It's Worth Doing

Going back to my (much used, dearly loved!) analogy of dressing successfully for a specific event, just as grooming and accessories can raise your look from "okay" to "Wow!" effective use of formatting elements can add polish and style to your resume, helping it to stand out among your competition. Going the extra mile to raise the bar on the appearance of your resume can also go a long way toward raising your response rate!

Career Champ Profile: Bill

Bill was aiming to make a career change from teaching to banking, so he developed a functional resume to support his job search goals. Some of the banks to which he was applying requested that he send a text version of his resume. After creating a resume in Microsoft Word, complete with many of the formatting elements we've discussed throughout this book, Bill then saved his document as a plain text file and added in some new formatting features. This document, though far less "pretty" than many of the other examples in this book, can be successfully submitted when a text version of his resume is requested.

Core Courage Concept

You're taking your career—and your resume—to the next level of performance. Adding in some of the formatting elements described in this chapter, whether they're bullets, lines, or even a photo, may feel awkward at first. Yet do your best to maintain a "Well, I'll try it and see how I like it" attitude at this stage in your resume development. Remember, *you can always change things back to the old way if you decide to!* Yet by getting past your old way of doing things, you greatly improve your chances for getting new and better results!

```
BILL SMEAD
2800 Longview Place
Fort Collins, CO 80526
(970) 222-6666, bsmeed@comcast.net

>>>>>TELLER / PERSONAL BANKER

STRENGTHS------------------------------------------------------------

Personable, detailed Customer Support Specialist with background in
preparing deposits and handling financial transactions in a business
environment; possess extensive customer service background with
strengths in problem solving and establishing rapport; proven ability
to work under pressure in a fast-paced environment while achieving
individual, team, and departmental goals; offer excellent written
communication skills; proficient in Microsoft Word, Excel, and Windows.

RELATED EXPERIENCE--------------------------------------------------

>>>Customer Service, Communication, & Teamwork Experience

* Background includes more than 10 years of experience in direct
customer support, including answering questions, solving problems, and
providing products and services.

* Possess multilingual skills (English, French, & some Spanish).

>>>Financial & Computer Skills Background

* Offer a proven track record for compiling and managing financial and
deadline details to support accurate, on-time achievement of goals.

* Experience includes preparing payroll and handling financial
transactions for multiple businesses.

* Passed security clearance to meet State of Colorado certification
processes.

* Skilled in Microsoft Word and Excel, with proven ability to learn new
programs successfully.

WORK HISTORY--------------------------------------------------------

* Substitute Teacher, Platte School District, 2005 - Present
* Property Management, Martin Apartments, 2002 - 2005

EDUCATION & LANGUAGE SKILLS-----------------------------------------

* B.A. History, Colorado State University, 3.4 GPA
* English & French (fluent), Spanish (partially fluent)
```

Figure 14.1: Bill's plain-text resume.

Confidence Checklist

☐ Make effective font choices.

☐ Work within the default margins in your word processing file.

☐ Choose an appropriate resume length.

☐ Add bolding, underlines, and italics to emphasize information.

☐ Highlight your position objective clearly.

☐ Apply effective use of graphic elements.

☐ Invest in quality resume paper in a neutral color.

☐ Use photos cautiously.

☐ Format your resume as "text only" when necessary.

Part 3

Create the "Extras" and Get Results

Chapter 15

Craft Cover Letters That Inspire Interviews

Whew! You've worked diligently to create a resume that will help you achieve your career goals, and now you're very close to being able to use this effective tool to advance your career. You have just one more important piece to put in place: your cover letter. In this chapter, you learn how to build a powerful, well-written letter of introduction using a proven step-by-step formula.

Risk It or Run From It?

- **Risk Rating:** Low to mid-range risk. By now, you're a pro at building effective job search documents!

- **Payoff Potential:** Because a cover letter is expected when you submit your resume, the payoff for creating it effectively is very high.

- **Time to Complete:** 30 minutes to an hour.

- **Bailout Strategy:** Check out the examples in this and other cover-letter books and make use of strategies you like instead of starting from scratch on your own. Or hire (or beg) someone else to write one for you.

(continued)

(continued)

- **The "20 Percent Extra" Edge:** By putting in the extra effort to produce a well-written cover letter, you lay the groundwork for increasing the results of your resume even more.
- **"Go for It!" Bonus Activity:** For additional ideas on how to write effective cover letters, ask recruiters to share with you some examples of a few they really like.

How to Create a Strong (Yet Simple) Cover Letter

You've worked so hard to develop a successful resume. Now, in a few easy steps, you'll learn how to write a cover letter that will serve as an effective introduction for the powerful resume you've created.

Use the Same Header as You Created for Your Resume

The name, address, and contact information header you've created for your resume will also work beautifully as the header for your cover letter. The result is a consistent, professional look.

Lead with an Effective Salutation

Someone once said to me, "The sweetest word to any person is his or her name." This same principle applies when creating the opening for your cover letter. I know this is true for me! I can be standing in a noisy crowd of people, intently focused on someone or some thing, yet the second I hear the name "Katy," my attention shifts. We love our names! And because we love our names so much, research shows that typically, readers of your letter will look at the salutation *first* to see whether you got this information correct. Considering this, whenever possible, it's in your best interest to use the name (correctly spelled!) of a decision maker in your cover letter salutation. How do you determine the names of those people involved in the hiring process? Here are a few tips:

- **Realize that in any hiring process, multiple people may be making decisions about you.** For instance, when you mail or e-mail your resume, a hiring coordinator typically will be gathering and organizing the submissions. This person may be an Administrative Assistant or a Human Resources specialist. The moment your resume lands on this person's desk or e-mail inbox, he or she instantly becomes a decision maker. "Hmmm, what should I do with this applicant? Is she worthy of making it to the next step in the process?"

  If your resume gets past the hiring coordinator, then it will most likely be passed on to another decision maker, such as head of the company or department in which you would be working. I'll refer to this person as the "hiring manager."

  In most cases, the hiring coordinator and the hiring manager are the two key decision makers in the resume review process. So, ideally, you will want to create and submit cover letters and resumes to *both* of these decision makers.

- **Attempt to get the names (and proper spelling!) of the decision makers.** Sometimes you can find a hiring manager's name on a search engine by inputting keywords such as "Vice President Sales Company X." However, information you find on the Internet may be out of date. For this reason, you will almost always need to make a phone call to obtain the names you need.

  When you call, make a request like this: "What is the name of the person who heads up the so-and-so function at your company?" You can then also ask, "And who is in charge of collecting resume submissions?" Be sure to confirm the spellings (and gender!) of any names you receive. Never, *ever* assume that you know how to spell a person's name. Chris Smith can be spelled as Ms. Chrys Smith, Mr. Chris Smyth, or some other way you and I have never even considered! And while you have someone on the line, confirm any professional designation, such as "Dr." or "Esq."

Panic Point! Career Cowards often cringe at the thought of calling a company to find out a hiring manager's name. "What if they yell at me and vow to never hire me!" Having made thousands of phone calls to companies in search of hiring managers' names, I've learned that in *most* cases, when you ask, you will be given the name quickly and painlessly. About 20 percent of the time, however, you'll run into a "gatekeeper" (often this is the receptionist) who will be unwilling to reveal a specific name. "I'm not authorized to give out that information," she may tell you. If this happens to you, don't sweat it. Simply say, "Thank you very much," and address your letter using a less personalized salutation, such as "Dear Hiring Manager." Or avoid making the call altogether by asking a friend to do it for you. And if a position advertisement specifically states "No phone calls," don't call!

- **If you're not able to get the decision makers' names, use a more generic salutation.** Here are some examples:

Dear Hiring Manager,

Dear Sir or Madam,

Dear Decision Maker,

While not nearly as effective as including decision makers' names, use of a generic greeting is acceptable.

Create an Introductory Paragraph That Clearly States Your Career Target

Often, writing the first paragraph can be the hardest part of putting together a cover letter. To make this task easier for you, here are a few openers that have proven to be very successful for other job seekers. Feel free to use them word for word, filling in the appropriate name or titles, or reword them to fit your personal style.

If you're responding to a specific position advertisement, this is an effective opening paragraph:

Your organization's outstanding reputation for excellence, along with my experience in **POSITION TARGET**, prompted me to submit an application for your current **POSITION TITLE** opening. Following are highlights of my background as they may pertain to your needs and requirements:

If someone that both you and the hiring manager know has recommended that you apply to a specific opening, include that person's name in the first paragraph. The name of a mutual acquaintance can greatly improve your chances for being called in for an interview:

CONTACT NAME, a mutual contact, told me about your company's current opening in the area of **POSITION TARGET** and encouraged me to apply. Following are highlights of my background as they may pertain to your needs and requirements:

If you have researched a specific company and are submitting a "cold" or unsolicited resume, this is an effective approach:

Having researched your organization, I perceive a potential match between my expertise in **POSITION TARGET** and the goals and mission of your company. Following are highlights of my background as they may pertain to your needs and requirements:

Articulate Your Key Strengths Quickly and Effectively

Having read, written, and tested thousands of approaches to cover letters, I've discovered that the KISS, or "Keep it Simple, Silly," approach is by far the best. Here's my secret formula for swiftly and successfully writing the main body of your cover letter:

- **Keep your focus on the key skill areas for the position.** Remember those from chapter 6? If you're applying to a specific position, they may be clearly listed in the job description. Otherwise, rely on the list of key skill areas you developed.

- **Write a few bullets that specifically address their key skill areas as well as your most important strengths.** Here's an example:

Experience in Operations & Team Management

    ✓   In my last position, I handled all aspects of business management, including employee hiring, development, and supervision; financial administration; and sales and service.

Track Record for Growing Revenues

    ✓   Under my leadership, the organization was able to grow from $150,000 to $2 million in annual sales within 4 years, largely due to my attention to establishing successful processes, cultivating excellent relationships with vendors, and ensuring a satisfying experience for customers.

Able to Work Independently

    ✓   My background and experience make it possible for business owners to confidently delegate management of the operation, knowing it is in capable hands.

> **Note:** You've probably noticed that, different from the resume verbiage examples I've provided you so far, I am using the pronouns "I," "My," and "Me" in the content for cover letters. You should write cover letters as if you're talking directly to the decision maker; therefore, the use of personal pronouns is appropriate.

- **Add in accomplishments and testimonials to build credibility and interest to your cover letter.** Remember the list of achievements you developed in chapter 9? These statements can also be added to your letter of introduction. You might also include testimonial statements you've received from coworkers (see the Career Champ example in this chapter). Don't have any testimonial statements to include? Then consider asking current or former bosses, team members, teachers, or customers to write some for you!

Panic Point! Career Cowards often ask me, "Why don't you include any character statements, such as 'I'm a hard worker, honest, and sincere.' Aren't these important in a cover letter?" Having read and experimented with many, many approaches to cover letters, I've determined that while *most* job seekers include the "I'm a hard worker, honest, and sincere," type statements in their cover letters, *hiring managers don't view those statements as being important or credible.* Why? Because (a) it's *assumed* that you will be honest and hardworking, and (b) because everyone else is including similar statements, your letter won't stand out in any significant way. In my opinion, your cover letter will be much stronger if you omit generalized character statements and instead communicate your strengths through concrete evidence examples such as achievements and experience statements.

Conclude Your Letter and Communicate Your Plan of Action

After you've created your cover letter's header, salutation, introductory paragraph, and key bullet statements, finish with a concluding paragraph that directs the decision maker to your resume and clearly states your desired next step. Here are a few examples:

> Please refer to my enclosed resume for additional details about my background. My goal is to locate an opportunity where I can apply my expertise to help a business grow and attain operational excellence. I welcome the opportunity to meet with you to discuss how my background may benefit your operation.

Or…

> Additional details about my background are included on the enclosed resume. To determine how my experience and qualifications may benefit your organization, I would welcome the opportunity to talk with you. In the next few days, I will follow up with you to confirm receipt of these materials and to determine a logical next step. Thank you in advance for your consideration of my interest and qualifications.

> **Note:** Job seekers often wonder if it makes sense to list the same experience statement or achievement in both their resume and cover letter. My answer to this question is a resounding "Yes!" As successful marketers have learned, repetition of important information is very effective. So don't be shy about including similar statements highlighting your strengths and accomplishments in both your resume and cover letter.

Note that in the second example, we've included a line stating that you will follow up in a few days. Following up on your submission can greatly increase your chances for landing an interview; *however*, you should include that statement only if you'll actually make the call. Otherwise, you may come across as someone unable to follow through effectively.

Sign It!

Believe it or not, about 25 percent of job seekers forget to sign their cover letters! So remember to add your signature before dropping your cover letter and resume in the mail.

P.S.: Use a Postscript to Draw Attention to an Important Aspect of Your Background

Remember my mentioning that a person's name is the first information he or she will read in a cover letter? Research also shows that a postscript statement, or P.S., is the *second* most read part of any letter. This provides you with a great opportunity to wrap up your cover letter with a "bang!" by including a P.S. that highlights something especially valuable about your expertise.

Keep Your Cover Letter to an Appropriate Length

The same guidelines I suggest for the length of your resume also apply to the length of your cover letter: One page is ideal, but two pages are acceptable, as long as your letter is filled with concise, relevant information.

Figure 15.1 is an overall outline of the cover letter suggestions I've just presented.

Your name, address, phone, e-mail somewhere on the letter, either in the header, in the footer, or under your signature

DATE

A contact name or
Hiring Manager
with address

Dear *NAME* or Hiring Manager:

I am writing to introduce myself and to apply to the position of **TITLE** as advertised in the **SOURCE FOR POSTING.** Following is a summary of my qualifications as they pertain to your position requirements:

An Ability to Operate XYZ Computer Systems (example):
- For the past 4 years, I have worked extensively with XYZ Computer Systems. Recently, I completed advanced training on XYZ and received a certificate of accomplishment. On my performance reviews, I have consistently received ratings of "Exceeds Expectations."

Write in Bold Word-for-Word One of The Requirements:
- *Respond here with a few sentences that specifically address the requirement. Ideas: Include length of experience, any special training or recognition; buzzwords that communicate you understand what the requirement entails. Keep statements concise and to the point.*

Another Requirement Would Be Listed Here:
- *Continue on down the page until you've addressed all the requirements—or at least those you can address.*

Another Requirement:
- *Don't worry if your cover letter goes past one page. As long as you're specifically addressing the company's needs, the hiring manager won't mind reading more than one page. And feel free to put the requirements in an order that best emphasizes your strengths—lead with your strong suit.*

Enclosed is a resume that details my experience and education. I welcome the opportunity to interview with you to discuss further how my background could be a fit for the **TITLE** position. In the next few days, I'll follow up with you to confirm receipt of this application and to determine a logical next step. Thank you for your consideration.

Sincerely,
Your Name—Be sure to sign your letter!

Figure 15.1: Cover letter suggestions illustrated.

Why It's Worth Doing

A participant in a seminar I once presented asked me, "Do I really need to send a cover letter with every resume I submit? My resume is already strong. Isn't that enough?" After thinking for a few

seconds, I said, "Technically, your resume *should* be enough. However, because most of the other candidates who apply will be including a cover letter with their resumes, if you *don't* include one, it will appear as if you don't care as much."

Another consideration about the necessity of cover letters is that while one resume screener may quickly scan your cover letter and then spend more time scouring your resume, a different resume screener will do the reverse, pouring over every detail of your cover letter and then skimming your resume. Because resume screeners have different review styles, it's important to cover your bases and submit both.

Career Champ Profile: Megan

Megan was in her third year of veterinary school and wanted to land an internship to support her goal of gaining hands-on experience. Because she had received a number of nice comments from former instructors, we were able to include these testimonials in her cover letter. We also included a P.S. to draw attention to Megan's volunteer and work experiences. The cover letter in figure 15.2 was especially effective in helping Megan stand out among other vet students seeking internship opportunities.

Core Courage Concept

With all the effort you've already put into creating your resume, you might be tempted to cut corners on your cover letter. Yet you know that a great resume submitted with a ho-hum letter of introduction will negatively affect your overall results. Instead, you've decided to spend the extra effort putting together a dynamite cover letter. Good for you! It's another small step toward achieving big career advances.

Megan Rockway

4236 Green Grass Way
Fort Collins, CO 80526
(303) 555-6666, mrockway@email.com

DATE

NAME &
ADDRESS OF
POTENTIAL
EMPLOYER

Dear Hiring Manager,

As a third-year student of veterinary medicine, I am writing to introduce myself and to express interest in any potential **Veterinary Medicine Internship/Externship** opportunities available with your organization. Following are highlights of my background as they may pertain to your requirements:

Achievements in Veterinary Medicine & Related Studies:

➢ Academically, I regularly receive top grades and ratings, ranking in the top half of my class within the #2-ranked veterinary teaching program in the United States.

Feedback from Others:

➢ I have consistently received positive feedback from my former employers and instructors, including these comments submitted as part of my graduate school recommendation letters:

✓ *"Megan finished in the top 1% of her class. She exceeds expectations to achieve a goal."* Troy Ebert, Assistant Professor, Colorado State University

✓ *"Megan maintains an extremely high standard of excellence in all her activities.... People follow her positive leadership style...."* J. Steven Moore, Assistant Professor, Colorado State University

Additional details about my background are included on the enclosed resume. I would welcome the opportunity to talk with you about any **Veterinary Internship/Externship** possibilities. In the next few days I will follow up with you to confirm receipt of these materials and to determine a logical next step. Thank you in advance for your consideration of my qualifications and interest.

Sincerely,

Megan Rockway

P.S. In addition to my academic studies, I have sought out and successfully completed several veterinary care volunteering and assistant assignments. Details of these are described on my resume.

Figure 15.2: Megan's cover letter.

Confidence Checklist

☐ Use the same header as you created for your resume.

☐ Lead with an effective salutation.

☐ Create an introductory paragraph that clearly states your career target.

☐ Articulate your key strengths quickly and effectively.

☐ Conclude your letter and communicate your plan of action.

☐ Sign it!

☐ P.S.: Use a postscript to draw attention to an important aspect of your background.

☐ Keep your cover letter to an appropriate length.

Chapter 16

Pull Together a Portfolio of Other Powerful Job Search Documents

Your resume and cover letter have been successfully created. In this chapter, you complete your portfolio of other job search documents, including your references listing and thank-you notes. You're in the home stretch…finish strong!

Risk It or Run From It?

- **Risk Rating:** Relatively low. These documents are easy to prepare as compared to your resume and cover letter.

- **Payoff Potential:** High. As companion tools to your resume, your references listing, thank-you notes, and portfolio will help move your job search forward more successfully.

- **Time to Complete:** 15 minutes to a few hours, depending on how much effort you want to put into each.

- **Bailout Strategy:** The references listing may be required—plus, it's very easy to put together—so I wouldn't ditch this one. You can skip sending a thank-you note (approximately 80 percent of job searchers don't bother!), but I recommend aiming to be in the top 20 percent instead. Creating an

(continued)

(continued)

accomplishments page or portfolio is definitely a "take it or leave it" activity, but if you're looking for additional ways to stand out among the competition, these documents may be worth your effort. At least read through the chapter to understand more about what I'm suggesting and then decide.

- **The "20 Percent Extra" Edge:** Putting together these important job search documents is a valuable activity that can definitely help you rise above your competition.

- **"Go for It!" Bonus Activity:** Organize your job search documents in both electronic and hard-copy filing systems so that you can quickly access the pieces you need as short-fuse opportunities pop up for you.

How to Create an Effective References Listing, Thank-You Note, and Portfolio

Now that you've created a resume and cover letter that will help you successfully achieve your career goals, complete your collection of effective job search documents with a well-written reference listing, thank-you note, accomplishments page, and portfolio. The following step-by-step guidelines make developing these documents fun and easy.

Collect Contact Information and Create Your References Listing

References are people who are able to personally vouch for your character and track record. At some time during the recruiting process, a hiring manager may request a list of your references to help him or her with decision making. These steps will help you pull together a list of references that will support you toward your job search goals:

- **Brainstorm a list of potential references.** Your references may come from a variety of sources, and you may choose to submit different reference names depending on the type of position you're targeting. For this reason, it's a good idea to brainstorm a long list of potential references that you can refer to and draw from over time. As a first step in creating your reference list, spend a few minutes brainstorming possibilities from the following sources:

- Former or current bosses and coworkers

- Teachers and instructors

- Vendors and customers

- Leaders and comembers of churches, clubs, or organizations

- Counselors or job search support specialists

- Long-time friends, acquaintances, and neighbors

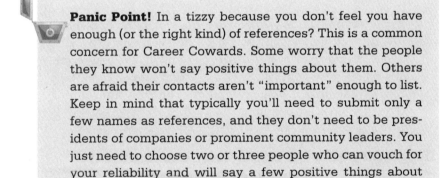

Panic Point! In a tizzy because you don't feel you have enough (or the right kind) of references? This is a common concern for Career Cowards. Some worry that the people they know won't say positive things about them. Others are afraid their contacts aren't "important" enough to list. Keep in mind that typically you'll need to submit only a few names as references, and they don't need to be presidents of companies or prominent community leaders. You just need to choose two or three people who can vouch for your reliability and will say a few positive things about you. Usually, once Career Cowards give themselves a little time to think through their list of potential references, they're able to identify the supporters they need.

- **Choose the best ones.** Consider the position for which you're applying and ask yourself, "Which of these people can best describe my expertise and character related to the key skill areas the position requires?"

- **Contact those individuals to confirm details and request their support.** After you've decided which reference names you want to submit, talk with all of them to verify that the contact information you have for them is correct, to gain their permission to be listed, and to inform them about the position to which you're applying. In this conversation, you can also let them know which aspects of your background to emphasize based on the requirements for the position.

- **Create a separate references document.** Use the header you created for your resume and cover letter and then list your references' names, contact information, and a statement about your relationship to them. Here's an example:

Lisa Pollard

Manager, Raster Technologies

(603) 555-2222

Lisa.pollard@rastertechnologies.com

Panic Point! "I don't want the hiring company to contact my current manager!" you may be worrying. You can avoid letting your current manager know that you're job searching by requesting that the hiring manager contact him or her *only* if you give permission first and *only* if there's a job offer pending.

Develop Follow-Up Notes That Communicate "Thank You, and I'm Very Interested!"

Most people know that a thank-you note is expected after a job interview, yet only about 2 in every 10 people send one. Why don't the other 80 percent? My guess is that (a) they're not sure what to write, and (b) they don't believe it's really that important. Yet in reality, thank-you notes can make the difference between being passed over for a job or moving to the next step in the hiring process! Here, I'll show you how to pull together a thank-you note quickly and successfully:

- **Create thank-you notes for key people in the hiring process.** These may include the hiring manager, hiring coordinator, as well as anyone else you may have interviewed with at the company. Although it's best to send individual notes to everyone, it's also acceptable to send a single note to the hiring coordinator and to request that he or she forward it on to the others.

- **Prepare your note as handwritten, typed, or in an e-mail format.** I personally prefer a brief, handwritten message on a simple, tasteful note card. Yet I understand that penmanship is a challenge for many job seekers, so a typed or e-mailed note is a better choice. Bottom line, the priority is to create and send the note; the format you choose should be based on your personal preference.

- **Include these three key pieces of information in your note:**

  1. Thank the interviewer for his or her time.

  2. State—or restate—why you believe you're a good fit for the job.

  3. Make it clear that you want the job.

  Figure 16.1 is an example.

  You may also want to include other details, such as a statement or two about a particularly relevant aspect of your experience that you forgot to mention in the interview.

- **Send your thank-you note as soon as possible after the interview, ideally within 24 hours.** If you don't get it sent that quickly, go ahead and send it anyway. A thank-you note sent later is better than not sending one at all!

February 11, 2008

Dear Rickie,

Thank you for interviewing me earlier today for the Customer Service Specialist position.

After talking with you about the position requirements, I'm even more convinced that I'd be an asset to your organization. My experience in client services will allow me to come up to speed quickly.

I look forward to hearing your decision regarding this position. The opportunity to work with you and the WellSpeed Company would be very exciting for me. Thank you again.

Sincerely,

Bob Brownard

Figure 16.1: A sample cover letter.

Develop an Accomplishments Listing or Portfolio to Make Your Resume Even More Effective!

Chances are, as you were developing your resume, you were reminded of several projects and achievements you've accomplished in your career. These successes can be compiled into an accomplishments page or portfolio to help you promote yourself successfully in job interviews. Here's how:

- **Compile a few of your most relevant accomplishments.** Put them on a single page using your standard header information, titled "Relevant Accomplishments," and listing 3 to 10 of the achievements you brainstormed in chapter 9. (Please also see the Career Champ example listed in this chapter.) In job interviews, you can make use of this handy tool when asked to describe an example of your expertise in a particular area. Simply glance at your accomplishments page for ideas! One of my clients came to refer to his accomplishments page as his "security blanket" because it increased his confidence so much. Be sure to take extra copies of your accomplishments page to share with your interviewer.

- **Present evidence of your expertise by creating a portfolio.**
Similar to the accomplishments page described in the preceding instruction, a portfolio is a collection of items that provide the interviewer with concrete evidence of your skills and successes. Here are examples of items you might choose to include in your portfolio:

  - Letters of appreciation from bosses, coworkers, or customers

  - A sample report, memo, or other example of your writing (be sure to mask any confidential information)

  - Photographs or drawings of products, plans, or projects

  - Certificates of completion for training programs

  - Any other items that will provide evidence of your expertise related to a key skill area for the job

  I strongly recommend choosing no more than 10 of your best examples to include in your portfolio. Too much of a good thing can be overwhelming to an interviewer!

You can present your portfolio in a range of formats:

- A slim leather (or leather-like) binder with clear plastic sleeves to hold your information

- An envelope-style folder with your examples held loosely inside

- An electronic Web-page portfolio to which you can refer the interviewer

Why It's Worth Doing

Spending a little extra time to create effective reference listings, thank-you notes, accomplishments pages, and portfolios can multiply the positive results of your resume. As an example, I was once involved in hiring an office manager. A colleague and I had interviewed five candidates for the job. Following the formal interviews, we were unanimous about whom we wanted to hire, and we made an offer to that candidate. She told us she'd let us know in two days.

In the meantime, another one of the candidates (not our first choice, but a strong contender) stopped by the office to drop off thank-you notes. She'd spelled all our names correctly (which is quite a challenge with a last name like mine!), and she emphasized her interest in the job. As it turns out, the candidate to whom we had made the initial offer ended up saying no. And guess whom we offered the job to next? The woman who had delivered the thank-you notes!

Career Champ Profile: Bryce

Bryce, an experienced hotel manager, was actively searching for his next position. Although his qualifications and experience are very strong, he still tended to get very nervous in interviews. To help boost his confidence, he created the accomplishments page in figure 16.2, which turned out to be an extremely comforting security blanket for him in interviews!

Bryce Walker   *General Manager*

1906 Mountain Top Drive
Fort Collins, CO 80524
(970) 333-7777, Bryce.Walker@gmail.com

Selected Accomplishments

- Oversaw operation of $2.5M hotel facility that achieved a top performance ranking from among 300+ facilities nationwide for growth, profitability, and customer satisfaction.

- Led property to top-performer status in market for 6 consecutive years through a dedicated focus on Continuous Quality Improvement.

- Achieved annual revenue growth averaging 8% per year in a highly competitive industry while attaining 42% profitability margins.

- Opened several hotels that earned top corporate ranking within the first year.

- Successfully managed a 40-hotel, $300M portfolio.

- Earned "General Manager of the Year" and "Hotel of the Year" awards from among a field of more than 300 contenders, based on significant revenue growth, 96.1% customer satisfaction ratings, and stellar leadership results.

Figure 16.2: Bryce's accomplishments page.

Core Courage Concept

Contacting and compiling references, writing thank-you notes, and creating portfolios and accomplishments listings are "take-your-career-to-the-next-level-of-excellence" activities that may feel new and awkward. Yet they *can* generate positive results, so you may be considering adding one or more of these tools to your collection of effective job search documents. You continue to grow and experiment as you find new ways to achieve your career goals. Kudos to you!

Confidence Checklist

☐ Collect contact information and create your references listing.

☐ Develop follow-up notes that communicate "Thank you, and I'm very interested!"

☐ Develop an accomplishments listing or portfolio to make your resume even more effective!

Maximize Your Resume's Results

All the hard work you've invested so far will begin to pay off for you now. Make the best use of your terrific job search documents by distributing them through the most effective channels. This chapter shows you how!

Risk It or Run From It?

- **Risk Rating:** There's moderate risk involved in some of these suggestions (but your "risk muscle" is probably pretty developed by now, right?).

- **Payoff Potential:** Colossal! Implementing just a few of the excellent suggestions in this chapter can skyrocket your career.

- **Time to Complete:** A few minutes to a few hours (depending on how motivated you are to get the best results out of your resume).

- **Bailout Strategy:** Leave your resume (the document you worked so hard to create) on your desktop and hope that a great employer comes knocking at your door.

(continued)

(continued)

- **The "20 Percent Extra" Edge:** Nine out of 10 job searchers do very little with their resumes, hoping that their dream employer will come looking for them. Yet you can significantly increase the results your resume generates by simply sharing it with some potential employers. Put yourself in the top 10 percent!

- **"Go for It!" Bonus Activity:** Some of these ideas may seem a little aggressive to you. Instead of writing them all off as too "out there," challenge yourself to try at least one of them.

How to Make the Best Use of Your Powerful Resume

You've worked hard to create your job search documents. Rather than let them gather dust, launch them into the world of work and move closer to achieving your career goals by using the following effective job search activities. Here are my top 10 favorites:

1. Customize Your Resume Every Time You Apply to a Job Opening

Now, thanks to the great resume foundation you've already built, modifying your resume will take you just a few minutes so that you come across as the perfect candidate for the job. Each time you apply to a specific job opening, tailor these components of your resume:

a. Job title: Simply plug in the position's job title, including any reference code or number if one is provided.

b. Keywords for the position: Using the process you learned in chapter 5 to create a keyword block, integrate keywords from specific job descriptions into the keyword section of your resume.

c. Key skills and accomplishments: As you update your keyword block using terminology from the position description, pay attention to the key skill areas described. Then make any changes to your key skills sections, especially if you're using a functional resume format, as described in chapter 12, or a hybrid format, as outlined in chapter 13. Also, add in or exchange descriptions of your accomplishments so that they emphasize your expertise related to the position.

d. Your cover letter: Modify your cover letter to include the position's job title, key skill areas, and highlights of your relevant experience.

2. Tap into Your Network to Identify Helpful Contacts in the Hiring Company

As you locate positions to which you want to apply, contact friends, family, current and former coworkers, and references to ask if they know of anyone connected to that company. When you locate people who may be able to help you, contact them to discuss the possibility of mentioning their name in your cover letter (some companies reward employees for recommending quality candidates), and ask if they would be willing to hand deliver your resume to the hiring manager. Lining up an advocate within the company can greatly improve your chances for being noticed and getting called in for an interview.

3. Submit Both Electronic and Hard Copies of Your Resume

Many companies now use online recruiting and application processes. In some ways, this makes things easier because resumes are automatically forwarded to e-mail inboxes or databases. Yet I'm hearing more and more that hiring coordinators miss receiving hard-copy applications—the paper cover letters and resume submissions they used to process by hand. They actually liked holding them, feeling the paper, putting them in piles. So, now I'm recommending that when you apply, send both electronic *and* hard-copy versions of your resume. Another note on this topic: In many, many instances I've known job seekers to follow up on the electronic applications they've submitted to make sure they were successfully received, only to discover that their resumes never made it to the company! For this reason alone, it's a good idea to send a hard-copy version as well.

4. Send a Second Submission of Your Resume Two Days Later

This suggestion is similar to the tip I just described, with one twist: Two days after you submit hard-copy and electronic versions of your resume (if the hiring company uses both methods), *mail a second hard-copy submission, using the same cover letter and resume,* and in the upper-right corner of your cover letter, handwrite

Second submission. I'm very interested.

For many of my clients, this simple step has significantly increased the number of calls for interviews that they receive. Why? Because when you send a second hard-copy submission, you wind up in two places in resume screeners' stacks of resumes. As they look through their stacks, they will see your resume *twice*, along with your hand-written message emphasizing your interest in the job. I strongly encourage you to try this technique to see how it works for you.

5. Play the Field

When you locate a position that looks appealing to you, multiply your chances for landing an interview by also presenting yourself to the company's competitors. Let's say, for instance, that you see a job position advertising for a chocolate taster for Bob's Yummy Chocolates. You like the sound of that, so you customize your resume and cover letter, submit both hard-copy and electronic applications, and then follow up with a second submission a few days later. In addition to all your application efforts to Bob's Yummy Chocolates, you also do some research into your local business directory and find that Bob has some competitors in town: Celia's Heavenly Cocoa Confections and Aunt Marge's Fabulous Candies. *Because you've already gone to the trouble of customizing your materials for one candy taster position, go ahead and send your resume to similar companies as well—even though they haven't advertised an opening!*

When one company is hiring for a particular specialty, it often means that their competitors will be, too. People within a particular profession may be shuffling around between businesses (as in Charlie, the chocolate taster at Bob's, decided to go to work for Aunt Marge's) or because there's an upswing in the demand for people with those skills. It's a bit of a domino effect—one change in the workforce can trigger several others—so be sure to capitalize on the opportunities!

6. Go Direct

Apply directly to companies where you want to work, even if there's no specific position advertised. This technique is called "direct application" and takes Tip #5 a step further. Studies show that one-third of all positions are filled through this avenue, yet (hint, hint) less than 10 percent of job searchers take advantage of it, so it has the potential to generate outstanding results for you! Simply identify 25 to 100 companies where you want to work (a target list) and mail your resume and a direct application cover letter directly to the attention of the hiring manager at those companies. (See an example of one of these letters in the Career Champ section of this chapter.)

Your phone book can be a helpful tool for creating your target list. Simply flip through the hundreds of industry categories in the yellow pages to identify interesting companies. Or talk with a reference librarian for recommendations on business directories and databases.

Panic Point! Career Cowards are often reluctant to mail their resume to an employer unless a position is advertised. "What if they think I'm being pushy and just throw my materials in the trash?" If this is a concern for you, consider these points: (1) Good managers are *always* on the lookout for great talent and are usually happy to spend a minute or two reading a resume of a potential employee; and (2) although most of the resumes you send *will* wind up in the trash (it's true—I admit it), your resume is *more* likely to end up in the trash when you apply to an advertised position because there's more competition! By applying directly to a greater number of potential employers, you actually *increase* the number of interviews you generate, bringing you closer to your career goals in a shorter period of time.

7. Ask for Help

Share your list of target companies with your supporters and ask for contact recommendations. Because you've gone to the effort to create a target list of potential employers, take things a step further by sharing this list with your friends, colleagues, and references. Ask them if they know of anyone at those companies whom you should contact and/or send a resume to directly. Again, knowing someone at a company can significantly improve your chances for landing an interview.

8. Try Again Later

If you aren't chosen for a job you really wanted, apply again with the same company six months later. Let's say that six months ago, you located a job announcement that looked like your dream position. You customized your resume and cover letter; submitted hard-copy, electronic, and second submissions; but ultimately weren't chosen for the job. Don't give up on this opportunity! Why? Because on average, *4 out of 10 new hires don't work out within the first six months.* Although they may not be fired, in 40 percent of the cases, the hiring manager is unhappy with the person chosen to fill the position. By mailing your resume, along with a short note like this…

Dear Hiring Manager,

A number of months ago I applied to an opening for a Chocolate Taster position with your company. I am still very interested in this position and ask that you will keep me in mind should you ever have a need for someone with my skills and background. I have enclosed a resume as a reminder of my experience.

I would welcome the opportunity to meet with you. Thank you in advance for your consideration of my qualifications.

Sincerely,

YOUR NAME

...you provide the hiring manager with a gentle reminder about you as a qualified candidate—and possibly the answer to his or her hiring woes!

9. Track Your Results

Monitor the results your resume generates, aiming for a minimum of a 10 percent response rate. On average, you can expect one call for an interview for every 10 applications you submit. If your resume is generating significantly fewer calls for interviews, attempt to troubleshoot the problem by asking yourself the following:

- Have I chosen a clear target for my resume?

- Have I included relevant keywords and developed my resume to emphasize my experience related to the key skill areas for each position?

- Have I followed the suggestions outlined in this book for how to most effectively present my work history, education, and other qualifications?

- Am I applying to positions that, in general, I am qualified to do?

- Am I customizing each resume to include the title for the position, along with any relevant keywords from the job description?

If you can answer "yes" to all these questions and are still achieving poor results with your resume, it could mean that you're aiming for positions that are especially competitive. In this case, it may make sense to aim for additional, less competitive career targets and develop and submit resumes to those positions as well.

10. View Your Search as a Numbers Game and Put the Odds in Your Favor

Over the years, I've talked with hundreds of job searchers who were frustrated with the results their resume was generating. "There must be something wrong with my resume," they usually say. Then I ask them, "How many positions have you applied to in the past three months?" "Oh, just a few, maybe four or five," they often reply. Considering that, on average, your resume will generate one call for an interview for every 10 applications you submit, applying to a position or two every month will make for a *very* slow job search. Improve your resume's results by sending out a higher volume of applications using tips suggested in this chapter. Ultimately, you'll move toward your career goals faster and more successfully.

Why It's Worth Doing

Just like a hammer, a resume is a tool that can help you get the job done. Yet if the hammer sits in a toolbox unused, it's worthless. Your resume, stuck sitting on your desk or in your computer, will do little for you unless it lands in the hands of decision makers.

About 90 percent of job searchers wait for positions to be advertised and then respond to them. While this isn't necessarily a bad thing to do, it does create a lot of competition, with 100+ job searchers applying to the same job. Although you may have a very strong resume (especially if you've followed the suggestions in this book!), it's still quite a feat for your resume to wind up in the top few that result in interviews.

To improve the results your resume generates, take advantage of the job search techniques that the 10 percent of the most effective job searchers use: Send your resume directly to companies that interest you, even if no positions are advertised. Show your target list of companies to your supporters and ask for recommendations of people at those organizations you should contact. And send your resume to the competitors of hiring companies to take full advantage of the resumes and cover letters you've created.

These simple steps will help you pull ahead of your competition, opening many doors for attractive positions that fit your unique skills and interests.

Career Champ Profile: Elsa

Elsa was motivated to find a challenging position in account management and sales as soon as possible. Rather than relying solely on job ads that would pop up occasionally on job Web sites and in her local paper, Elsa created a list of nearly 50 potential employers that seemed interesting to her. Then she mailed her resume with the cover letter in figure 17.1 to those companies, even though no specific openings were advertised. This approach generated four job interviews.

Core Courage Concept

After you've worked so diligently to create a strong resume and cover letter, it would be a shame not to use it to its full advantage. Even though it may feel scary to promote follow-up with a second submission to an open position or to present yourself directly to a hiring manager at a target company that seems appealing to you, doing so allows you to take full advantage of your resume's potential. Sure, you'll run into some rejection, and many of your resumes will wind up in the trash. Can you handle that? Of course, you can! It helps to remind yourself that job search is a numbers game, and the more of those dynamite resumes that you put in the hands of decision makers, the faster your results and career will progress.

Elsa Martin   *Business Development—*
508 Mary's Lake Road   *Account Manager*
Fort Collins, CO 80525
(970) 222-9999, e.martin@email.com

DATE

NAME &
ADDRESS
OF POTENTIAL
EMPLOYER

Dear Decision Maker,

    I am writing to introduce myself as a potential **Account Manager / Business Development** resource for your organization. Having researched your company, I perceive a potential match between my strengths and your organization's future growth. Following are highlights of my background as they may pertain to your development objectives:

> ➢ For 10+ years, I have successfully cultivated, managed, and grown profitable relationships with key accounts in the media and fulfillment service industry. My track record in these efforts has been impressive:
>
>> o **My accounts frequently grow by up to 40% annually** through identification, proposal, and implementation of value-enhancing products and services.
>
> ➢ I possess extensive knowledge of media / print production processes, and am constantly driven to learn new technologies and processes to enhance profitability and customer value.
>
> ➢ For organizations looking to grow profits through expansion into international markets, my expertise in this arena is strong:
>
>> o With both my present and former employer, **I significantly increased business revenues through expansion into multinational territories.**
>> o To foster successful multicultural communication, I am **fluent in English, Spanish, and French**, as well as other languages.

    Additional details about my background are included on the enclosed resume. To determine how my experience and qualifications may benefit your organization, I would welcome the opportunity to talk with you. In the next few days, I will follow up with you to confirm receipt of these materials and to determine a logical next step. Thank you in advance for your consideration of my interest and qualifications.

Sincerely,

Elsa Martin

Figure 17.1: Elsa's cover letter.

Confidence Checklist

☐ Customize your resume every time you apply to a job opening.

☐ Tap into your network to identify helpful contacts within the hiring company.

☐ Submit both electronic and hard copies of your resume.

☐ Send a second submission of your resume two days later.

☐ When you locate a position that looks appealing to you, multiply your chances for landing an interview by also presenting yourself to the company's competitors.

☐ Apply directly to companies where you want to work, even if there's no specific position advertised.

☐ Share your list of target companies with your supporters and ask for contact recommendations.

☐ If you aren't chosen for a job you really wanted, apply again with the same company six months later.

☐ Monitor the results your resume generates, aiming for a minimum of a 10 percent response rate.

☐ View your job search as a game of numbers and put the odds in your favor.

Check Out Sample Resumes
for Additional Ideas

Throughout this book, you've had a chance to learn about many different approaches to writing resumes that will move you toward your career goals. To help you even further, I've provided this collection of sample resumes, representing individuals with a wide range of career objectives and backgrounds. Feel free to borrow ideas to create your own excellent job search documents!

Cory Hughes   *Mechanical*
                                                   Engineering/Design

1700 Redstone Street
Loveland, CO 80537
(970) 888-2222, e-mail: coryh@comcast.net

A**ccomplished, experienced Mechanical Engineer/Designer** with expertise in 3D modeling with SolidWorks (> 4500 hrs), and design of optomechanical and injection-molded assemblies, parts, and fixtures; skilled in mechanical design, thermodynamics analysis, optical alignment, and design of stable optomechanical systems; adept at prototype construction with electrical, optical, and mechanical components; possess strong mechanical design skills, including extensive experience with medical product design and manufacturing development.

Work History

Mechanical Engineering, MedInstruments, Inc., 1999–2007
Developer and manufacturer of medical diagnostic products. Position responsibilities:

- Used RIM, machining, centerless grinding, chemical polishing, electropolishing, vacuforming, drawing, EDM, extrusions, abrasive flow, and micromachining to produce mechanical and optomechanical assemblies and parts.
- Monitored and complied with ISO 9001, CDRH, safety, clinical, and international regulations.
- Researched, sourced, verified, and validated diode and gas lasers; assembled, integrated, and performed acceptance tests on flow cytometers.
- Investigated, tested, and validated various mounting techniques, including elastomeric bonding, mechanical, and hard bonding; specified and evaluated optical coatings, especially dichroic.
- Wrote test procedures, investigation reports, verification and validation plans, risk analysis and mitigations, and product specifications.
- Evaluated systems for production and R&D, and performed troubleshooting and repair.
- Initiated and completed ECOs in response to cost reduction requests, increased functionality, reliability concerns, and obsolescence issues with vendors.
- Initiated, evaluated, maintained, and managed vendor relationships.
- Established cross-functional teams to solve difficult problems.

Sample Engineering & Design Projects...

- ✓ **Instrumentation Product Development:** Designed and built several mechanical parts and systems, flow cell, optomechanics, and molded parts for CyAn Personal Flow Cytometer.
- ✓ **Red Diode Upgrade:** Laser-changed mounting style and introduced peltier cooling into custom package to reduce positional instability, wavelength drift, power loss.
- ✓ **Flow Cell Improvement:** Designed and implemented improved flow cell in product. Researched surface energies of various materials to reduce bubble adhesion.
- ✓ **Optomechanical Mounts Redesign:** Redesigned original mounts to reduce cost (up to 70%), increase pointing stability, decrease assembly time, and satisfy user requests.
- ✓ **R&D Project Liaison:** Worked in Denmark for 2 months after merger to establish R&D relationships, train teams on new products, and establish further development plans.
- ✓ **Float Switch Failure Analysis:** Led investigation of float switch failures, resulting in new specifications, custom part development, performance validation, and field upgrade.
- ✓ **Product Container Enhancement:** Re-created part and assembly drawings in Solidworks, and collaborated with vendor to make improvements, including chemical-resistant labeling.
- ✓ **Camera Component Redesign:** Created a high-resolution camera assembly to improve alignment of the lasers to the core stream.

Figure A.1: Cory had the challenge of showing his qualifications as an engineer, without having an official degree. Referring to his most recent job title as a "role" (Mechanical Engineering) rather than a job title (Mechanical Engineer), while also highlighting engineering project accomplishments, helped achieve this goal.

Cory Hughes
Resume, page 2 of 2
(970) 888-2222, e-mail: coryh@comcast.net

Additional Work History

➤ **Full Time Student,** *Colorado State University*, 1995–1999
➤ **Mechanical Engineering Design,** Hitek Solutions, 1997–1998
➤ **Technician,** CSU Veterinary Teaching Hospital, Nuclear Medicine, 1994–1996
➤ **Opto-Electronics Technician,** United States Air Force, 1990–1994

Position details provided on request.

Additional Engineering Projects

'66–'77 Ford Bronco—All modifications extensively tested, documented, and provided to other users for duplication.

423ci Smallblock Ford Motor—*Designed, sourced, and built smallblock Ford motor for particular requirements of rockcrawling-custom heads, custom block, reprogrammed SEFI system for fuel/air delivery. Documented progress and provided to other users.*
Twister Wristed Radius Arm—*Designed, developed, fabricated, and tested (5 iterations) suspension component, allowing high levels of articulation with minimal user assembly.*
Redesigned entire electrical system—*Designed, documented schematic, sourced, and fabricated new wiring harness for entire vehicle, adding functionality and reliability.*
Designed new steering restraints—*Developed a kit for consumers for more durable wheel location for rockcrawling while improving stock streetability.*
Founded Bronco Registry of Northern Colorado—Two chapters still going today.

Education, Associations & Professional Development

- Bachelor's Studies, Colorado State University

- SPIE (International Society for Optical Engineering) Coursework:
  o SC013—Principles for Mounting Optical Components (Yoder, Jr.)
  o SC014—Introduction to Optomechanical Design
  o SC015—Structural Adhesives for Optical Bonding
  o SC219—Materials: Properties and Fabrication for Stable Optics

- Additional Engineering Coursework:
  o MCAD of Denver courses in SolidWorks Sheetmetal, SolidWorks Advanced Assembly Modeling, COSMOS FloWorks, COSMOSWorks Professional (member of COSUG)
  o Advanced Excel Training
  o Geometric Dimensioning and Tolerancing (GD&T) —ANSI Y14.5M
  o Electronics Technical Training, United States Air Force

Disabled USAF Veteran requiring no special accommodations—details on request.

Joe Jobsearcher   *Software Project Manager*
3333 Red Fox Rd.
Ft. Collins, CO 80526
(970) 555-1111, joe.jobsearcher@comcast.net

Effective, experienced **Software Project Manager** with proven track record for leading complex technical projects toward successful completion. Adept at planning, directing, and coordinating the needs, tasks, and workflows of projects; overseeing data preparation for any new major project; and interfacing with management and customers to prepare cost analyses, recommend priorities, and generate schedules. Experienced in monitoring status of projects to stay within cost and completion guidelines. Possess in-depth knowledge of software development cycle and industry standards and techniques. Offer a proven track record for coaching and mentoring high-performing teams to achieve mutual and individual goals.

WORK EXPERIENCE

Program Manager, Software QA, Hewlett-Packard Company, 2003–current........................
Manage incoming defect streams for concurrent HPUX enterprise software releases.

- Collaborate across software development projects to meet schedule and quality goals.
- Represent the software lab at daily defect review meetings to assess the overall fitness of each HPUX release.
- Mediate cross-functional "swat" teams to solve critical defects.
- Debug kernel crash dumps to determine root causes, and forward defects to lab teams for fixes.
- Manage transition from legacy defect tracking system to HP standard defect tracking system:
    - ✓ **Currently transitioning 200,000+ active and archived defects.**
- Act as liaison to assess overall fitness of HPUX releases.

Project Manager, Software Engineering, Hewlett-Packard Company, 2000–2003................
Led, developed, and maintained enterprise applications and environments through software life cycle.

- Led 17 engineers to investigate, design, deploy, and support installation system for HP OpenView enterprise management product line.
    - ✓ **All phases of product delivery came in on time and within 10% of extremely tight budgetary constraints.**
- Bridged gap between IT and R&D, managing the daily build process through allocation of engineering resources across seven geographically diverse sites as well as four autonomous software development labs.
- Partnered with Quality Assurance, Information Engineering, Operations, Product Development, Global Support, Current Product Engineering, Technical Marketing, Expert Centers, Contract Negotiations, and Human Resources to define and implement project plans.
- Worked closely with all levels of management from technical leads through R&D Vice President to deliver software projects and implement best practices and processes throughout engineering.
- Led, managed, and delivered a 3-year project focused on the creation of a revolutionary source code exchange system between Hewlett-Packard Company and Hitachi Inc.
    - ✓ **Avoided escalations through continual hands-on management of HP's and Hitachi's leadership teams.**

Continued...

Figure A.2: Joe was aiming for two different job search targets simultaneously: 1) Software Developer, and 2) Software Project Manager. For this reason, we created two separate resumes, including job titles and aspects of his background that were most relevant to each.

Joe Jobsearcher
Resume page 2 of 2
(970) 555-1111, joe.jobseacher@comcast.net

Software Solutions Architect, <u>Hewlett-Packard Company</u>, 1999–2000..............................
Created solution architecture for the HP-Cisco-Software.com Unified Communications project.

- Managed technical partner relationships across functional and corporate lines.

Senior Software Engineer, <u>Hewlett-Packard Company</u>, 1995–2000...................................
Used C++ and design patterns to develop e-mail-based communications transport technology,
spanning HPUX and NT operating systems with a single source stream.

- Developed and delivered cross-platform, completely reusable Object-Oriented software library
  extensively used to track and monitor object lifetimes within C++ libraries.
    - ✓ Several customers integrated library into products to provide "live" monitoring and
      tracking of software objects in released software, enabling support labs to
      troubleshoot software.
- Presented seminars to R&D labs on creating cross-platform code reusable libraries.
- Earned reputation as lab-wide expert on C++ and design patterns.

- ➢ **Possess additional expertise in Perl, C, C++, Pascal, AWK, LEX, YACC, Java, KSH—**
  Details on request.

EDUCATION & CERTIFICATIONS

- **B.S. Computer Science**, Montana State University
- Microsoft Visual C++/MFC certifications
- **Advanced education** classes:
    - ➢ Dynamic Leadership
    - ➢ Attracting, Hiring, and Keeping Great People
    - ➢ Technical Leadership
    - ➢ Project Management Fundamentals
    - ➢ Advanced Object-Oriented Methods using C++

- **Language training:**
    - ➢ 3 Months German
    - ➢ 3 Months Japanese
    - ➢ 3 Years French

Joe Jobsearcher *Software Developer*

3333 Red Fox Rd.
Ft. Collins, CO 80526
(970) 555-1111, joe.jobsearcher@comcast.net

Experienced, accomplished Software Developer with excellent analysis, problem solving, and debugging skills; experienced in developing product requirements consistent with customer needs and industry standards; adept at ensuring coherency and consistency between software projects; able to adapt quickly to changes in priorities, circumstances, and direction; skilled in establishing and maintaining effective relationships with colleagues and customers; self-starter with ability to exercise judgment, perform assigned tasks, and meet schedules; possess technical expertise in the following:

> ➢ C++ programming on various operating systems (Windows/UNIX)
> ➢ RDBMS (Oracle/Sybase/DB2/Informix/Postgres/MySQL/SQL Server/ODBC)
> ➢ Experience with C interface database programming
> ➢ Windows NT/2000/XP/2003
> ➢ UNIX platform programming
> ➢ Experience with cross-platform development
> ➢ 64-bit operating systems (Win64, Linux 64, Solaris, AIX, HPUX)
> ➢ C++ reusable component/library development
> ➢ Experience with maintaining large-scale testing infrastructures

WORK EXPERIENCE

Software QA, Hewlett-Packard Company, 2003–current...
Monitor and manage incoming defect streams for concurrent HPUX enterprise software releases.

- Collaborate across software development projects to meet schedule and quality goals.
- Mediate cross-functional "swat" teams to solve critical defects.
- Debug kernel crash dumps to determine root causes, and forward defects to lab teams for fixes.
- Manage transition from legacy defect tracking system to HP standard defect tracking system:
    - ✓ Currently transitioning 200,000+ active and archived defects.
- Act as liaison to assess overall fitness of HPUX releases.

Software Engineering, Hewlett-Packard Company, 2000–2003.......................................
Developed and maintained enterprise applications and environments through software life cycle.

- Determined direction, gathered requirements, defined project scope, and prioritized activities.
- Partnered with Quality Assurance, Information Engineering, Operations, Product Development, Global Support, Current Product Engineering, Technical Marketing, Expert Centers, Contract Negotiations, and Human Resources to define and implement project plans.
- Performed risk analysis and contingency planning to ensure on-time product delivery.
- Designed, deployed, and supported a new installation system across the HP OpenView enterprise management product line.
    - ✓ All phases of product delivery came in on time and within 10% of extremely tight budgetary constraints.
- Supported development of revolutionary source-code delivery system between Hewlett-Packard Company and Hitachi Inc.

Continued...

Figure A.3: Joe's second resume.

Joe Jobsearcher

Resume page 2 of 2
(970) 555-1111, joe.jobseacher@comcast.net

WORK EXPERIENCE (continued)

Software Solutions Architect, Hewlett-Packard Company, 1999–2000.................................
Created solution architecture for the HP-Cisco-Software.com Unified Communications project.

- Managed technical partner relationships across functional and corporate lines.

Senior Software Engineer, Hewlett-Packard Company, 1995–2000...................................
Used C++ and design patterns to develop e-mail-based communications transport technology,
spanning HPUX and NT operating systems with a single source stream.

- Developed and delivered cross-platform, completely reusable Object-Oriented software library
  extensively used to track and monitor object lifetimes within C++ libraries.
  - ✓ Several customers integrated library into products to provide "live" monitoring and
    tracking of software objects in released software, enabling support labs to
    troubleshoot software.
- Presented seminars to R&D labs on creating cross-platform code reusable libraries.
- Earned reputation as lab-wide expert on C++ and design patterns.

  - ➤ **Possess additional expertise in Perl, C, C++, Pascal, AWK, LEX, YACC, Java, KSH—**
    Details on request.

EDUCATION & CERTIFICATIONS

- **B.S. Computer Science,** Montana State University
- Microsoft Visual C++/MFC certifications

Charlie Comster

Organizational Development
Specialist

316 Lovely Road
Fort Collins, CO 80525
(970) 222-1111, account@email.com

Experienced, effective Organizational Development Specialist skilled in evaluating many complex, interrelated factors, ranging from technology and processes to culture and reward systems, toward achievement of organization objectives; able to engage with individuals at all levels of an organization about specific issues, diagnose business performance challenges and opportunities, and facilitate solutions through to completion; possess strengths in creating organizational change plans that support the business strategy; background in coaching business leaders, building knowledge networks across organizations, and growing partnerships; proven track record for successfully coordinating, managing, and driving multiple projects.

WORK HISTORY & RELATED QUALIFICATIONS

- ➢ **Business Development Strategist,** Hewlett-Packard, Imaging & Printing Group, 2000–2006
- ➢ **Program Manager/Customer Support,** Hewlett-Packard, Consumer & Retail, 1998–2000
- ➢ **Manager,** Hewlett-Packard, North American Marketing Center, 1996–1998
- ➢ **Business Analyst,** Hewlett-Packard, Information Storage Americas, 1994–1996

Additional Work History Provided on Request

Organizational Development Experience..

- • Proven strengths in translating organizational development objectives into concrete, effective strategies, achieving desired results while maintaining high team morale.
- • Adept at helping individuals develop the capacity to successfully adapt to change.
  - ✓ *Example:* Implemented change-management program resulting in successful transition of division responsibilities and team members into new assignments.
- • Highly skilled at group and individual communication, including developing and delivering effective presentations to support organizational change initiatives.
- • Possess outstanding ability to understand and diagnose organizational challenges, and to develop and implement effective strategies to improve profitability, productivity, and morale.

Business Strategy Expertise..

- • Offer extensive background in leadership and management, including working with teams to define and implement change initiatives and achieve business objectives.
- • Business expertise includes working with international divisions and business partners, maintaining and improving profitability, and monitoring all aspects of operational processes.
- • Expertise in accounting supports a proven ability to integrate fiscal and organizational development objectives with attention to bottom-line results.

EDUCATION

- • **M.S. Accounting,** Colorado State University
- • **B.S. Microbiology,** Colorado State University

Figure A.4: Charlie was making a career change from her background in business operations to work as an Organizational Development Specialist. For this reason, it made sense to present her information in a functional format, focusing the majority of the resume content on experience and accomplishments that pertained to her new career goal.

Charlie Comster

Customer Service

316 Lovely Road
Fort Collins, CO 80525
(970) 222-1111, account@email.com

Experienced, personable Customer Service Specialist with proven track record for understanding customer needs, making product recommendations, and delivering outstanding customer service; proven track record for successfully handling customer inquiries and resolving customer issues; able to work effectively both independently and as part of a team; skilled in multitasking and maintaining poise in high-stress situations; possess excellent communication and analytical skills; offer strengths in attention to detail and organization; skilled in MS Office: Word, Excel, PowerPoint, and Access.

WORK HISTORY

Customer & Business Support, Hewlett-Packard, Imaging & Printing Group, 2000–2006
- Supported customers and team members in multiple locations to implement business strategies and achieve desired results.
- Monitored several aspects of business operations, including financial, sales, and service, to ensure attainment of quality and profitability objectives.

Customer & Program Support, Hewlett-Packard, Consumer & Retail Services, 1998–2000
- Worked with team members to design effective retail operation processes.
- Developed in-depth understanding of effective customer service principles and practices.
- Monitored financial aspects of the division to ensure accuracy and profitability.

Team Leader, Hewlett-Packard, North American Marketing Center, 1996–1998
- Managed group of marketing specialists.
- Worked with team to improve customer rebate program.

Marketing Specialist, Hewlett-Packard, Information Storage Americas, 1994–1996
- Implemented numerous marketing programs to promote business products.
- Helped improve internal business processes to achieve greater efficiency and profitability.

Payroll/Petty Cash Supervisor, Hewlett-Packard, Accounting Services, 1993–1994
- Managed team of payroll specialists.
- Ensured accurate and timely processing of payroll and petty cash requests.

Financial Analyst, Hewlett-Packard, Disk Memory Division, 1991–1993
- Analyzed financial and tax information to support manufacturing activities.
- Implemented new automation systems to improve efficiency.

Additional Work History Provided on Request

EDUCATION

- **B.S. Microbiology,** Colorado State University
Additional graduate work in accounting studies. Details provided on request.

Figure A.5: We wrote this resume to "tone down" Charlie's background so that he could apply for a variety of positions.

Marlee "After"   *LCSW, ACSW, RN*

316 Lovely Road
Fort Collins, CO 80525
(970) 222-1111, account@email.com

Experienced, effective Licensed Clinical Social Worker possessing RN and ACSW
credentials; highly experienced in providing direct social work services to patients, families,
and staff to ensure needed assessment intervention, support, and referral; adept at coordinating
services with agencies and other team members, and responding to information and referral needs
of the community; offer a broad experience background obtained through service in a variety of
environments and populations.

WORK HISTORY & EXPERTISE

➢ **Psychotherapist/Clinical Social Worker**
   Naval Hospital Camp Pendleton/Naval Medical Center 2004–2008
➢ **Case Manager/Psychotherapist**
   Poudre Valley Hospital/Mountain Crest/Senior Counseling Group, 2003–2004
➢ **Case Manager**
   Interfaith Behavioral Health/Jewish Family Service, 1999–2002
➢ **Registered Nurse**—*Details provided on request*

Expertise with Therapy & Treatment Modalities...

- Offer 10+ years of experience providing assessment, case management, and therapy to
  address depression, anxiety, panic attacks, domestic violence, and other issues with
  patients.
- Possess extensive expertise administering and interpreting biopsychosocial assessments,
  developing treatment and discharge plans, and advocating for patients and families.
- Experienced in providing crisis intervention and ongoing therapy to support individuals
  experiencing Post Traumatic Stress Disorder. *Example*:
  - ✓ Supported Marines at Camp Pendleton using cognitive-behavioral therapy,
    guided imagery for relaxation, eye movement desensitizing and reprocessing
    (EMDR) therapy in processing traumas, and continued assessment to monitor
    suicide and homicide ideation.

Specialized Populations Background..

- Offer a proven track record supporting the elderly, Marines, adolescents, and families
  with effective therapy and treatments.
- Work experience includes successful therapy delivery in military, hospital, hospice,
  healthcare, agency, and residential treatment environments.
- Also offer extensive background in understanding medical terminology and healthcare
  issues as a result of RN experience.

EDUCATION & LICENSES

- **Master's in Social Work**/Bachelor's in Social Work, *San Diego State University*
- **Registered Nursing**, *Southwestern College*
- LCSW—CO/993017 (Current); RN—CO/162692 (Current)
- EMDR Parts 1 & 2; Mediation Training

*Figure A.6: Marlee had the challenge of overcoming a "hoppy" job his-
tory, where she worked a few months at one location, a few months at
another, and so on. To present a more cohesive perception of her work
history, we listed multiple employers on one line, under a single job title.*

Katy Piotrowski

Marketing Specialist

3000 Sycamore Lane
Fort Collins, CO 80524
(970) 555-2222 katy@jobworksco.com

Experienced, accomplished **Marketing Specialist** with proven track record in planning, implementing, and monitoring a wide range of effective marketing activities; possess knowledge of advertising, direct marketing, public relations, web promotions, and event planning; proficient in Microsoft applications including Word, Excel, PowerPoint, Access, and Publisher; able to work effectively both independently and within team environments; consistently receive excellent feedback from coworkers and group leaders.

WORK EXPERIENCE

- **Marketing Projects Coordination,** FUMC, 2000–Present (part time)
- **Team Leadership/Project Coordination,** NCL, 2002–2006 (part time)
  Additional work experience in teaching and customer service; details provided on request.

Marketing & Project Coordination Expertise..

- Background includes proven experience working with organizations to conceptualize, plan, and implement a wide range of marketing programs.
  - Organized and implemented a successful promotional event that exceeded revenue-generation goals; handled planning, promotion, and coordination of 100+ people.
  - Researched and wrote detailed document outlining more than 20 no-cost marketing resources available to the organization—along with contact names and how-to steps—allowing team members to easily and effectively make use of marketing services.
  - Developed annual promotional event schedule, leading to a 75% increase in marketing activities and a significant growth in new business.
- Completed numerous marketing courses as part of college curriculum; won top honors in regional marketing contest.

Teamwork & Computer Skills...

- Possess more than 5 years of experience working successfully in teams. *Example:*
  - Applied effective teamwork skills to pull together ideas and needs of a diverse team, resulting in a communications plan to expand membership within nonprofit organization.
- Offer knowledge of several computer programs, including word processing, database, and graphics applications; able to learn new programs quickly.

EDUCATION & COMMUNITY INVOLVEMENT

- **B.S. Communications,** University of Tennessee
  Additional graduate coursework in counseling; details on request
- Poudre School District—*Volunteer*; First United Methodist Church—*Membership team co-chair, Teacher*; National Charity League—*Volunteer*

Figure A.7: Yes, this is one of my own resumes! It's written based completely on volunteer work that I've done, demonstrating how you can successfully represent unpaid work experiences on a resume.

Index

A

accomplishments
  brainstorming, 107–108
  examples of, 103–104
  including in resume,
    102–103
  writing accomplishments
    page, 186–187
achievements
  brainstorming, 107–108
  examples of, 103–104
  including in resume,
    102–103
  writing accomplishments
    page, 186–187
address in resume header, 54
affiliations
  brainstorming, 108–109
  examples of, 104–105
  including in resume, 103
  whether to include, 109
associations
  brainstorming, 108–109
  examples of, 104–105
  including in resume, 103
  whether to include, 109

awards
  examples of, 105
  including in resume, 103
  whether to include, 110

B

background
  experiences inventory,
    creating, 24–28
  as resume key element, 5
  what to include, 62–68
bold (in resume), 159
boxes (for highlighting), 161
bullets
  keyword block as, 53
  usage of, 160

C

career change
  Education section, what to
    include, 94
  sample resume for,
    210–211
  showing work history
    for, 81

electronic version of resume, submitting with hard copy version, 193

expanding work history, 126–130

experience
    lack of, in key skill areas, 140
    lack of, in work history, 82
    what to include, 62–68

experiences inventory
    creating, 24–28
    matching with key skill areas, 65–68, 139–142

extras
    in chronological resumes, 130
    in functional resumes, 142
    including in resume, 102–111
    reasons for including, 111
    selecting for resume, 106–111

F
focus of resume, 34–40
following up, 176
fonts, selecting, 156–158
formal education
    lack of, in Education section, 93–94
    listing, 91
functional resumes
    creating, 136–142
    described, 117
    importance of, 143
    outlining, 136–138

as part of hybrid resumes, 149–150

sample of, 210–211

functions versus job titles, in work history, 83–84

G
gaps in work history, 80–81
general resumes versus specific resumes, 35–36
graphic elements, 160–161

H
hard-copy resume, submitting with electronic version, 193
header
    for cover letter, 170
    for resume, 54–56
highlighting
    with boxes, 161
    career target, 159–160
hiring managers
    obtaining names of, 171–172
    resume-reading scenario, 18–20
    what they want, 12–18
hobbies
    examples of, 105
    including in resume, 103
    whether to include, 110
hybrid resumes
    chronological section, creating, 148–149
    described, 117